"Clear"

"Dr. Harvey makes it abundantly clear that children with
access to a well-structured early learning program can
develop extraordinary intellectual capabilities. Not only that,
but these children are often wonderfully aware of life's
possibilities and socially well-adjusted, to boot."

Masaru Ibuka
Founder and Honorary Chairman
Sony Corporation

"Crucial"

"Kids Who Start Ahead, Stay Ahead makes the crucial point
that the way to get children ready for school
is to feed their minds."

Fred M. Hechinger
Former Education Editor of
The New York Times

"Essential"

"This is an essential book. It uncovers a buried treasure
chest that may well contain the answer to the nation's
educational crisis. Dr. Harvey presents compelling evidence
that very young children when exposed to a specific
early learning program excel when they reach school."

Ralph Pelligra, MD
Space Medicine
National Aeronautics and Space Administration

"Vitally Important"

"Written expressly for parents, beautifully, clearly, free of jargon, Dr. Harvey's *Kids Who Start Ahead, Stay Ahead* furnishes an impressive amount of first-hand evidence that very young children who have been exposed to an appropriate early learning program will do fine once they reach school. Vitally important."

Professor Omar K. Moore
Inventor of the "Talking Typewriter"
University of Colorado

"Encouraging"

"It's amazing how much we neglect our most important national resource—babies—by minimizing their capabilities. Dr. Harvey and his colleagues are, indeed, performing the most needed work in America today—educating, encouraging and believing in parents helping their babies to learn."

Lauren Robinson-Brown
Reporter
Boston Globe

"Stimulating"

"Dr. Harvey's constructive and stimulating book, *Kids Who Start Ahead, Stay Ahead*, will kindle enthusiasm in every parent and educator concerned with the social challenges of the nineties."

Dr. Charles Lee
Literary Critic
WFLN, Philadelphia

Kids Who Start Ahead, Stay Ahead

WHAT ACTUALLY HAPPENS WHEN YOUR HOME TAUGHT EARLY LEARNER GOES TO SCHOOL

Dr. Neil Harvey

Avery Publishing Group

Garden City Park, New York

Cover design: Rudy Shur and William Gonzalez
In-house editor: Karen Hay
Typesetter: Bonnie Freid
Printer: Paragon Press, Honesdale, PA

Grateful acknowledgment is hereby made for quotations
reprinted by permission of
The Smithsonian Magazine (March, 1984),
TIME Magazine (January 11, 1963),
Glenn Doman (*How To Multiply Your Baby's Intelligence*,
Avery Publishing, 1994),
And, of course, all of the mothers and fathers who so
generously wrote of the experiences of their early learners
when they went to school.

Library of Congress Cataloging-in-Publication Data

Harvey, Neil
    Kids who start ahead, stay ahead : what actually happens when your
home-taught early learner goes to school / by Neil Harvey.
        p. cm.
    Includes bibliographical references (p.) and index.
    ISBN 0-89529-614-4
        1. Gifted children—Education (Preschool)—United States. 2. Home
schooling—United States. 3. Institutes for the Achievement of
Human Potential. 4. Mainstreaming in education—United States.
5. Educational acceleration. I. Title.
LC3993.218.H37   1994   94-3961
371.95—dc20   CIP

Printed in the United States of America

10   9   8   7   6   5   4   3   2

Contents

Appendices

To Florence, my wife of forty-four years,
whose inspiration and unflagging support
charged my life with meaning,
who did not live long enough to witness this book,
which is truly a product of her devotion.

A Word About Gender

There are no chauvinists at The Institutes, either male or female. We love and respect both mothers and fathers, baby boys and baby girls. To solve the maddening problem of referring to all human beings as "persons" or "tiny persons," we have decided to refer to all parents as mothers and all children as boys.

Acknowledgments

This book would never have seen the light of day had I not heard Glenn Doman declare, more than three decades ago, that human beings had more brain than could be used up in ten lifetimes, and that, pitifully, we were letting so much of it go to waste.

His words and his ideas, like missing squiggly-shaped, interlocking jig-saw puzzle pieces, fit neatly and snugly into empty spaces in the philosophical panorama I'd been fabricating since early teen years, a construct of ambitions and goals best summed up in the question: "What do I really want to do with my life?"

No words, of course, can adequately express my gratitude to Glenn, only a few years my chronological senior, who has influenced me with beneficent strength of father, teacher, and warm, staunch friend.

My deep thanks to Richard Mitchell for his wonderfully wise allegory of the bears, "The Bear Truth," which enhances our book.

It is true that, without the Directors and Staff of Child-Brain Developmentalists of The Institutes for the Achievement of Human Potential, this book would never have been possible. Their one hundred and fifty per cent dedication to the children of the world, unparalleled by any other staff I've ever met, fills me with admiration and gratitude. They are the teachers of the parents who, after taking the course How To Multiply Your Baby's Intelligence have gone on to rear the stunningly intelligent children who are the subject of this book.

How grateful I am to them all: Katie Doman, our founding mother; Janet Doman, Director; Douglas Doman, Vice-Director; Roselise H. Wilkinson, M.D., Medical Director; Alan Sosin, M.D., Assistant Medical Director; J. Michael Armentrout, Director of Special Projects; Susan Aisen, Director of the Institute for Intellectual Excellence; Miki Nakayachi, Vice-Director of the Institute for Intellectual Excellence; Matthew Newell, Director of the Institute for Physical Excellence; Ann Ball, Director of the Institute for Physiological Excellence; and their Vice Directors, Phyllis Kimmel, Intellectual Excellence; Rosalind K. Doman, Physical Excellence; Dawn Price, Physiological Excellence; Elaine Lee, Director of Children's Affairs; Janet Caputo, Director of the ETI Off-Campus Program; and the superb staff of Child-Brain Developmentalists: Teruki Uemura, Carol Newell, Dr. Ernesto and Thaisa Vásquez, Marlene Marckwordt, Thaya Nesadurai, Erik and Rumiko Doman, Catherine Ruhling, Communications Director; Nest Holvey, Assistant to the Chairman, each of whom freely and patiently responded to my incessant requests for help. A special kudos to Jim Kaliss, Art Director, for his unstinting advice, suggestions, and innumerable favors, well beyond the call of duty or even genuine friendship.

For more than a decade, Masaru Ibuka, Honorary Chairman of International Sony Corporation, and Kenneth Nees, President, Sony Corporation of America Foundation, have awarded generous grants to The Institutes to support the Evan Thomas Institute's annual Intellectual Enhancement Projects, the primary beneficiaries being the young students who are awarded scholarships to the Evan Thomas Institute's International School, our private academic school, licensed by the Commonwealth of Pennsylvania. These young people are our in-house "Renaissance Children."

I acknowledge with deepest appreciation the astute advice I received from Rudy Shur, Managing Editor, and Karen Hay, Editor, Avery Publishing

Group, and from Lee Pattinson, Institutes' Director of Publications and Liaison Officer for Australia. She generously benefited me with many suggestions arising from long experience as prize-winning author and editor, and she scrupulously vetted the manuscript.

I would like to thank Min Berg, supremely intelligent friend who, cautioning me all too frequently, read every line through the eyes of those for whom this book is intended: parents, parents who do not wish to read jargon or psychobabble which, as a professional educator, I adore spouting from time-to-time, just to keep my hand in.

Mostly, I am indebted to the parents who cooperated by responding to our questionnaires. Their experiences with their own children, their observations, and their conclusions are more authentic and meaningful than those of any professional person when it comes to reporting about the delight of raising their own children, those charming kids who have started ahead and are staying ahead.

Foreword

There are hundreds of thousands, possibly millions, of young parents today, and you may be one of them, who are denying their babies an opportunity to achieve their unbelievably high potential. They are waiting until their tiny children go to school before letting them in on the secret of reading, of doing math, of learning how to play a musical instrument, of participating in physical activities.

One of the most powerful reasons for the delay is a concern, born of a stubborn long-standing myth that one would be "wasting time," that once the children reached school, all earlier efforts, no matter how much fun was involved, would be in vain. The myth holds that once children get to school, even though they know how to read, how to do math, how to speak a foreign language, how to engage in physical routines, they would become just like everybody else, like all of the other kids who didn't start early to learn to read.

After working with more than thirty thousand parents and their children during some forty years, our staff at The Institutes for the Achievement of Human Potential recognizes the myth for what it is: a dreadful lie. Particularly disturbed is our Dean, Dr. Neil Harvey. He had a solid background in education when he joined our group of Child-Brain Developmentalists back in the early sixties. Here he acquired insights in infant neurophysiology that made him extremely sensitive to the terrible harm being perpetrated by this hurtful myth.

He resolved to do something about it, and I'm glad he did.

Ever since my book *How To Teach Your Baby To Read* was published back in 1964, I must have appeared on more than two hundred network and local television and radio programs. On nearly every occasion, the talk show host, a member of the studio audience, or a telephone caller-in, asked me the question, phrased something like this:

"Yeah, but what's gonna happen when my kid gets to school?"

The question was also posed by many of the

thousands of young mothers and fathers who have attended The Institutes' course, How To Multiply Your Baby's Intelligence. Obviously, these parents weren't as intimidated by the myth as the television objectors, since they had come to learn as much as they could about how to give their children their fleeting chance at excellence. These parents had come from all of the States of the Union and all the continents of the world. They were not to be put off.

In *Kids Who Start Ahead, Stay Ahead,* Dr. Harvey destroys the myth once and for all. How? He approached the very people who had helped their tiny children to become intellectually, physically, and socially excellent. The parents themselves. He asked these experts what actually happened when their kids got to school. He felt that the parents, who knew their own kids better than anybody else in the world, would provide honest answers as to how their children fared once they had entered the grades. From their comments, he knew he would shed the light of truth on underlying, bothersome concerns such as, "Were they bored?" "Were they shunned by their playmates?" "Did they turn out to be little nerds?" "Did they forget the love and warmth and joy of learning with their mommies and daddies?" "Did they fulfill the predictions of the doomsayers and become stolidly mediocre, just like everybody else?"

This book provides a ton of hard evidence, evidence in the form of reports from the parents of more than three hundred children, parents who had helped their babies and toddlers learn many wonderful survival skills at a time of life while they were still able to learn with great joy and without even trying. Dr. Harvey reports what actually happened to these early learners when they got to school—what happened to them intellectually, physically and socially. A great portion of the book consists of the parents' first-hand accounts.

This book will be welcomed by parents who are confused because of those noxious myths, some born of oddball stories about those rare mothers who have taught their little babies as if they were in a school classroom, unaware of the different quality of instruction that takes place while engaged in the early-development program with a tiny child.

At this time in America's history when all clear-thinking leaders and citizens agree that "our educational system is in shambles," and that our "nation is at risk," surely we must make a major change in the way we prepare the next generation to meet awesome challenges.

When we read what actually happens to early learners when they get to school, the direction of that change seems inevitable. We become convinced that the "Gentle Revolution" will indeed occur in the very early years.

In my opinion, the very important question, "What's going to happen when my child gets to school?" is answered most convincingly by the parents whom Dr. Harvey quotes liberally. They are the very people who have lived day-in and day-out with their kids from the moment of birth, wondering at every step whether to obey their most natural instincts (to allow their babies to learn as much as possible as early as possible), or to heed the wagging fingers of the myth-propagators.

May I propose that you read ahead and draw your own conclusions?

Glenn Doman
Founder of The Institutes

Preface

For as long as I can remember I have been obsessed with the subject of early learning. I have wondered how it happens, what it means, and how important it may be.

When, in 1963, fourteen years after undergraduate school, I returned to the University of Pennsylvania to work for a Ph.D. in early education, my thesis homed in on the subject of early reading. I wrote and produced 195 half-hour TV programs, *Wordland Workshop,* the purpose of which was to study how successfully parents might be able to help their three-year-old children to read with the help of television. That program was based on the best-selling book *How to Teach Your Baby to Read* by Glenn Doman.

Glenn had invited me to be director of the teaching institute of The Institutes for the Achievement of Human Potential. I couldn't resist the unequaled opportunity to satisfy my hunger to understand early learning *first hand*.

About early learning, a vast number of questions intrigued me. At The Institutes, I learned the answers to many of them. Especially, I learned that the secret may be that, uncannily, the human brain, that most marvelous mysterious machine, anticipates the need for its owner to survive in this crazy world. During the first months of life, the density of synapses (the microscopic clefts between brain cells) increases sharply. Then, a mysterious winnowing takes place, and at one or two years of age, wonderful opportunities for rapid, easy learning reach some kind of climax. Brain cells, however, continue to multiply, but at an appreciably slower rate each day, until, by the age of six, new cells have all but ceased to appear.

It is tempting to speculate whether the purpose of such an abundance of synapses and rapid growth of cells explains the astonishing ability of a tiny child to learn *anything* so quickly and effortlessly. It is certain that a different *quality* of learning is taking place during those very early years, a quality of learning that enables the new human being to master an entire language by two years of age. Or, to gain command of two, three, or more languages.

This wondrous learning facility pertains to all human babies, all over the world. For example, in the jungle, a primitive child might learn to hurl a stone at an edible bird on a branch; in our "civilized" culture, a toddler may become proficient in reading and instant math. Or, just as easily learn to play the violin.

With the passing years, as my professional career progressed, I realized that the ancient counsel, "Let kids be kids!" doesn't really mean letting them run loose. It really means that we have to appreciate the need of those kids to satisfy a fierce urge to learn, to learn everything needed for survival in our demanding grown-up world.

That adult world presents an economic environment where it is crucial to know how to read, to write, to compute, to be aware of our incredibly technological culture. Perhaps more important, to enter that world as mature human beings, our children must acquire the ability to empathize, to be sensitive to the needs of others; in other words, to enjoy social competence. Success in school and life depends on how well our children have learned their lessons. Success and independence and a sense of fulfillment is what all loving parents want for their children.

For these parents, this book has as its purpose the provision of important background information, especially if they wonder what effect early stimulation will have on their tiny children later in life.

That this laudable curiosity be satisfied with reasonable and dependable data, I wanted to ask those mothers and fathers who did indeed already follow their parental instincts, and thereby equipped their babies in a superb way for life. Still, even these folks, in significant numbers over the years, before beginning their early development program, have mused, "It sounds reasonable to me, that's why I intend to help my child learn so many things, but what's going to happen when it's time to go to school?"

In order to obtain an impeccable "scientific" answer to that question, we would have to mount a "controlled study," that is, we would have to find two groups of parents and children who, for all intents and purposes, had the same characteristics. Both groups of children would come from an identical "population." The experimenter would make sure that the group who will be early learners are matched on a number of important criteria with the children who will wait until they go to school before being exposed to reading and math and foreign languages, etc.

Both groups would have essentially the same number of boys and girls of the same age, race, religion, and level of health; they would come from families with the same number of brothers and sisters; their parents would have the same amount of education, the same cultural interests, and the same economic status. The investigator would also consider the results of pretests that establish levels of "maturity" as a part of the matching procedure.

We would call one group, the "experimental group." These children would receive an early development program provided by their parents, while another, nearly identical, group, the "control group" would be treated just like everybody else.

At the end of the study, we would test both groups and see whether the early development program had made any significant difference in their function, that is, whether the kids in the experimental group did better in school than the children in the control group. We would try to learn whether they did better intellectually (in school subjects), physically (in games and athletic play), and in social areas (how they got along with their peers and elders.) If post-tests show that the experiment has produced results better than those achieved by conventional education, *results that may not be ascribed to chance,* the new system may be considered to be superior to the conventional one.

It is not appropriate here to discuss the vast complications of such a highly technical exercise, but it is important to point out that to conduct a truly "scientific" controlled study in education is virtually impossible. At least, that's the opinion of the eminent educational research authority, Deobold B. Van Dalen. In his book *Understanding Educational Research*, he declares, "As a result of. . . practical and ethical problems and the complexity and nonuniformity of human phenomena, the experiment in the social sciences is not possible in the same sense that it is in physics and chemistry."

Van Dalen suggests, instead, a viable alternative to the "insurmountable" (Van Dalen's word) problem of experimental control in education. He proposes, "For controls, oft-times the rest of the world would have to do, i.e., those children who were following more or less conventional practices in respect to the age at which they started."

We have opted to follow Van Dalen's advice, and have conducted a questionnaire survey, intending to compare the accomplishments of home-taught early learners with "those children who were following more or less conventional methods in respect to the age at which they started," meaning, of course, the other children of the same age in their classes.

Accordingly, in 1988 we made contact with 239 families who had attended the How to Multiply Your Baby's Intelligence course in the late seventies and early eighties. They were parents who had carried out a reasonably effective early development program in years before their children entered school. Subsequently, they responded with reports about their 314 children (144 girls and 170 boys) who are currently attending school.

These parents, who represent all walks of life, were obviously proud of their accomplishments, and in their comments, their pride shone through. They have furnished a cogent response to the question: "What actually happened when my home-taught early learner went to school?" They have told us in their own words how their children fared in handling school subjects, how they performed on the athletic field, and how they got along with their peers.

Throughout the text, we will emphasize that these are real everyday kids we are speaking of, not just percentages, the sort of cold statistics you find in many studies purporting to be scientific. We won't speak of little S2, rather we'll mention the child's name, and have mother tell you what *actually* happened. Near the end of the book, we'll tell you how several home-taught early learners made out after they graduated from school and went out into life.

And that, in so many exciting ways, is why we ventured forth upon this quest.

The Bear Truth

by Richard Mitchell

Often, especially when my life and work as a teacher seem empty and vain, I tell myself a story about bears. Bear cubs are born in the early spring. There are usually two of them. For five or six weeks they are utterly helpless, blind and bare. When they are ready, their mother takes them out into the world and shows them its ways. She keeps them close for as much as two years, and the little family wanders here and there, finding food and good places to spend the night, just as the cubs will have to do themselves when they are grown. They learn, I have to guess, what is good to eat, and what isn't, what prey is worth chasing, and what can't be caught by bears. They learn to fish and to raid the hives of the bees. And their mother is always near.

She has good reasons for keeping them close. For one thing, it isn't easy to be a successful bear; there are many skills to learn if the cubs are to stay alive. And, for another, their lives are indeed in peril. Male bears are also wandering here and there looking for food, and they have no moral or social objections to eating bear cubs. They do, however, seem to have more sense than to fight with the mother of cubs for what would be, after all, only one small meal.

I have heard that mother bears teach their cubs the equivalent of a fire drill in school. She will surely fight any male who comes near her cubs, and she would probably win, but she would obviously fight better could she know that the cubs were safely out of the way. So she teaches them to scamper up the nearest tree at a certain signal. Climbing trees is the one thing at which the cubs are better than the grown-ups. She often sends them up a tree just for practice, and lets them stay there for a while before she calls them down. It seems prudent, and I like her for it.

On a certain day in the spring of the cubs' second year–how does she choose it?–she calls a drill. Up they go. And there they wait. And wait. And wait. Does she look back? I don't know. But, little by little, she wanders away and disappears into the underbrush. She will never come back. I see, as in a dream, her cubs, waiting and wondering, listening for a signal, an all-clear that will not come. The evening falls, and still they wait. They look at each other, and they look at the darkening earth below, and no one calls them down. At last, of course, they must come down. They must go into the world, each his own way, alone. Now they are really bears.

In fact, I know very little about bears. And my story is probably more generalized and romantic than the facts would always justify. But I do know a little something about teaching, enough to believe that if I as a teacher could do my work as well as a mother bear does hers, then I would not often find it empty and vain.

Happily, the culture of the bears will never change. As

long as there are bears in the woods, mothers will fitly rear their cubs for the life of a bear in the woods. But if I suppose the utterly improbable, what prospect appears? Imagine that, for some very good reason, the mothers of cubs find it impossible to put in two whole years of hard service. That little by little they cut from their curriculum this or that little thing, and, driven by nothing less than the inescapable demands of other duties, hand over to the general community of bears much of the work that they are no longer able to do. What then will become of the cubs?

Something like that is now our case, and it would explain many unhappy conditions. Our culture changes always. In these days, the mothers of our cubs are very busy. The times are hard and growing harder. Merely to feed the cubs, the mothers must leave them behind and travel far from home. They have to hand over to the general community of our kind the whole nurture of the young, and, should they find it inappropriate or even pernicious, they cannot simply take it back into their own hands; they must rather become activists seeking change and reform in the general community itself, a slow and uncertain process.

And so they have, what with PTA meetings and campaigns and petitions to politicians, even less time for the cubs. At last, they have to give it all up, hoping for the best, hoping that somehow or other, the work that was meant to be done out of love will get itself done out of compromise and consensus among the countless contending forces of the ever-changing body politic.

At the heart of the book you are about to read, there is a symbolic image of extraordinary power. I have seen it myself, in a dizzying multitude of representations in the office of Glenn Doman. It is the image of the Mother and Her Child. It is a recurrent icon in every human culture, and so potent a message that we can read it even in a photograph of the bear and her cubs.

The bond between the mother and her child is the irreducible nucleus of all other human bonds, for it is the only self-evident human bond that there is. Since the meaning of fatherhood is well-known to us, we imagine that the family is also a self-evident bond, but it isn't. Fatherhood had to be discovered, and the mother and her child were a holy icon long before that discovery. From the nuclear bond, all the others have been generated by custom and convention, the family, the clan, the tribe, the state, the great world of humanity itself. It is out of what Shakespeare cannily calls "the curiosity of nations" that we know of clubs and parties and second cousins once removed. The heart and model of all human bonding is the mother and child.

It is obviously the job of the mother bear to bring her cubs into what we might call the fullness of being a bear. That is surely a large and complicated business, but it is probably not infinite. We can name and count the habits and skills that make what we would call "a good bear," a bear who does well at what a bear should do. But where are the boundaries of the fullness of being a person? When we can read and write and cipher pretty well, when we can write a letter that makes some sense, when we can fill out the forms, when we can make a living at some sort of work, when we can eat a balanced diet and purchase prudently, where, exactly, do we stand in relation to all that we could do? Does anyone ever stand at the farthest limit, beyond which there is no going? This is a great dilemma of human life, from which the bears are excused: We can not suppose ourselves infinite, but neither can we know our limits. Still, we must come down out of the tree into the falling night, and live.

This is of course the great idea that informs this book and the work of The Institutes in general—that we can always be more than we are. It is coupled here with what seems to me a great realization: that education, the continuous process of breaking out of boundaries, is fueled by love. At some level, we all know that it is love alone out of which we can make each other—and ourselves—better than we are. That, surely, is why every incipient schoolteacher with whom I have ever spoken—and there have been many—has claimed as motivation for choosing what is in fact a routinely unrewarding career, the love of children. Even when they don't even know any children, they claim to love them. They are supposed to. It's just talk. But it reveals that they also know that to do their work they should love the children. Nobody loves children. "Children" is a concept, not a person. Loving requires this child, right here and now, in the flesh.

This is why there is no teacher like a mother; she is, as I think William Bennett once said, the best possible department of health, education, and welfare. It has been the remarkable achievement of the people at Glenn Doman's Institutes, obviously inspired by his own remarkable achievement, that they have been able to love their children as a mother would. It can happen. Thus, they have often worked seeming miracles which aren't truly miracles at all. A mother bear could do the like if she had to, but she doesn't have to. She knows when enough is enough. But we, for whom there is no enough, can indeed work such seeming miracles—out of love.

There is a frightening imperative in this book, and there will be many, I think, who would excuse themselves. The education that it commends is not a trick, not a stunt, not a gimmick, and not—oh, most especially not—an "innovation." It is old, very old. It is a call to hard labor, a labor so private and personal that no society will pay for it, and a labor so hard that no salary can buy it. It is, in a phrase that we often use but apparently never think about, a labor of love.

Introduction

Aren't things okay the way they are? Shouldn't we be satisfied? Why read early? Why learn math at such a tender age? Why multiply intelligence? Why acquire encyclopedic knowledge before three? Why become more physically capable? Why learn to play the violin, be introduced to world's culture, refine social graces, speak foreign languages, and do ballet—all before going to school? *Why?*

For three basic reasons: First, and literally vital, there's the fact that the speedily growing brain of the newborn baby and tiny child is super-receptive to sensory stimulation. While the child-brain developmentalists of The Institutes for the Achievement of Human Potential have known about the enormous capacity that babies have for new facts for nearly half a century, two scientists, Chiye Aoki and Philip Siekevitz, have reported on their December 1988 study in the *Scientific American.* They stated, "The final wiring of the brain occurs after birth and is governed by early experience." They had demonstrated in the laboratory that the brain responds to sights, sounds, tactile sensations, tastes, and smells by growing *physically*.

The Institutes' fun-filled early-learning program, carried out by a baby's loving mother and father, thickens the myelin sheath of a tiny child's naked nerve fibers, and makes that insulation more protective. Thus shielded, nerve fibers increase their conducting efficiency, and send messages from the outside world to the brain faster, easier, more accurately. Glenn Doman pointed out long ago that when frequent, intense, and long lasting messages reach working brain cells, they tend to increase the very young child's ability to receive visual, auditory, and tactile information.

Larger, healthier, more efficient brain cells receive, retain, and act upon ever-greater quantities of information. They do their job better. They enable the new little human being to learn more, and to learn more easily. He'll have greater stores of information on tap. Thus prepared, he will not only meet and overcome personal challenges more successfully, but hopefully, he will develop the brain power needed to solve the kind of awesome problems now threatening the future of our planet and, just as important, create wondrous new ways to enhance and fulfill our human experience.

The second reason for learning to read early—and to do math and the rest—is that infused as the brief sessions advocated by The Institutes for the Achievement of Human Potential are, with the joy and love that only a child's parents can provide, it's the *natural* thing to do. It's easy and amusing! It's a jolly game, not an obligation or a chore, as learning facts often gets to be during primary and later grades in school.

The Institutes' team has learned that in the same way that the sucking reflex drives an infant to drink milk, a baby automatically soaks up facts when they are presented *appropriately.* After he's got the facts well stored, he takes advantage of enhanced opportunities for exploring and testing and coming to his own conclusions. The result after four or five years: a young person who, upon entering school, is a scholar in every sense of the word.

The third reason is that, by attaining intellectual, physical, and social excellence early, the little child achieves a higher level of our practically infinite human potential; he becomes admirably equipped to help design and bring about a better world for all of us.

Since 1978, The Institutes for the Achievement of Human Potential has presented the course, How to Multiply Your Baby's Intelligence, to more than 3,000 mothers and fathers of tiny well children who have come to Philadelphia from all the states of the Union and 107 countries on all five continents. These parents have learned how to help their very young children reach levels of performance undreamed of by either our civilized or primitive ancestors, even those wonderfully talented early humans who inhabited the Lascaux caverns in southern France.

Back in 1991, I traveled to the French Dordogne region to see the heralded and truly magnificent cave paintings. With a group of gaping tourists, I stood in semi-darkness and wondered at the luminous drawings, prehistoric masterpieces by stone-age Michelangelos. As an Institutes' child-brain developmentalist, I tried to imagine what a typical cave family was like, how parents and children used to spend the time of day, and particularly, how the young were raised. I stared at colored sketches of aurochs (prehistoric cows), antelopes, deer, horses, and other animals that ranged the plains of the dim reaches of time past. I marveled at the brilliance of the artists, untutored geniuses, who had painted those antique creatures.

In my mind's eye, I traveled back 30,000 years to the open mouth of a cave near an ancient body of water, a vision bathed in bright sunshine. Several nude women, one who was pregnant, were seated near a blazing fire. They were scraping and pounding some leather hides. On the back of one female an infant in a leather sack was loosely but firmly draped. Several children of four, five, and six were engaged in helping the grown-ups at their task. Just within sight outside on the grass, two younger tykes, about three years old, were tussling and scrapping.

For no reason apparent to anyone else, the mother reached around and retrieved her baby. She studied the child briefly and then began nursing. Obviously, she had received some kind of wordless message from her baby; she was "tuned-in."

In the middle of the cave floor I spotted a wee toddler, nearly a year old, walking and falling, getting up, attempting to grasp a thorny stick, dropping it, holding on to a boulder, then walking and falling again. She was completely nude and moved in utter freedom, unrestricted by any garments. The earthen cave floor had been beaten smooth by bare feet for hundreds of years. It was not slippery. The little one, unshod, enjoyed a large uncluttered area to practice her ambulation; she was frolicking in a torrent of tactile sensations, the warm solid ground, the cold hard rock, the prickly brambles on her toy branch; she was on her way to becoming a big girl.

Then I dwelled on the tiny children scuffling at the cave's mouth, and visualized the titillating experiences of their daily lives. They lived always on the edge of survival. If they were lucky, they would make it to twenty years of age; if even luckier, they would become the elders of the tribe at thirty. Yet during the very quick-passing time of their babyhood, they were absorbing everything that would be required to subsist in their primitive environment: language, social skills, techniques for learning. They were benefiting from culture passed on from generation-to-generation since human beings became human.

The longer these little children were able to remain in their initial environment, the stronger it would affect them. As human fledglings, they had the longest childhood of any animal species. They were passing through the most sensitive period of their lives. They were absorbing knowledge of the tools and techniques of their people. If they didn't learn these vital lessons during this critical phase of striking plasticity, they probably would not live out their first decade. Learning while they were still very young—at three, four, and five years of age—they would attain needed flexibility, and store up a vast range of options that would equip them to meet and beat a host of life-threatening challenges.

Still woolgathering, I realized that the culture of these cave dwellers was not only different from that of our children as we near the twenty-first century, but also much simpler. Their basic culture had not changed for thousands of years while our Western culture has been utterly transformed in just five hundred years. We've speeded from the agricultural age through the industrial revolution to the unbelievable atomic age. The current upward spiral of information is like an atomic blast. In the past hundred years, the expansion of information has zoomed up in a nearly vertical curve. And all that new knowledge may ultimately find its home in the human brain.

The human brain—it is there that our story begins.

1

How I Became
a Child-Brain
Developmentalist

*No more than perhaps 125,000 cells are present in
the beginning. But eventually they will multiply
into some one hundred billion neurons that are the
basis of all functions of the brain.*

Richard M. Restak, M.D.
The Mind

W hat would you say if I told you someone
could live with only half a brain?"

I thought this was an unusual question. I studied
the face of my companion. I wanted to make sure
he was serious. Even though twinkling blue eyes
capped a bright smile, he was not kidding.

We had been introduced only thirty seconds
before. We were seated beside each other at the
head table of a donor dinner sponsored by the
Jacob K. Sandler Link #34 of the Order of the
Golden Chain. The charity event had pre-empted
Palumbo's night club on a Sunday evening in the

spring of 1957. My wife, Floss, had arranged the evening and, though I find such affairs tedious, I was obliged to attend. She explained that the grant recipient that evening was the Rehabilitation Center at Philadelphia, and the Director, Glenn Doman, had lots of interesting ideas. She promised to seat me next to him.

And there he was, crew-cut sandy hair, ruddy complexion, stocky build, about forty-years-old, smiling, waiting for an answer to his question.

The night club din hampered two-way communication. That, of course, didn't prevent people from talking. Everybody was talking. It was just that nobody was listening. Listening was impossible.

Glenn repeated the question. This time, only a few inches from my ear. "What would you say if I told you someone could live with only half a brain?"

Piercing the hubbub, I hollered, "Either you'd be kidding, or else you'd be talking about some kind of miracle."

Glenn chuckled, then shouted, "No, I'm not kidding, and I'm not talking about some kind of miracle, at least, not in the generally accepted sense of 'miracle,' as something marvelous that happens for which we have no explanation. It is a miracle, though, of surgery. It's called 'hemispherectomy.' Only the most skilled neurosurgeons can do it. And they resort to it only in the most extreme circumstances. A patient has to be suffering from a paralysis on one side of the body, intractable seizures, and be on the point of dying."

He raised his voice a notch to reach me through the clamor, "And not only do many patients survive this drastic operation, but I can show you survivors who go on to lead normal, or near normal lives. One little girl I know, with only half a brain, has a measured IQ of 160!"

"My God!" I was fascinated beyond belief. My wife hadn't misled me.

Glenn was about to continue, but we had to pause for the welcoming speech and the blessing. Then, dinner. I can't recall the entrée. The speeches have vanished. Even Glenn's acceptance talk fades. I think he spoke of how the money was going to be put to a good cause.

All other recollections of that evening have faded into the mists of eternity; what I do remember of those hours nearly a lifetime ago is our screaming interchange above the uproar. We jabbered while we ate. The after-dinner speeches muzzled us. We looked at each other, pained.

Topics Glenn managed to touch upon ranged from the vivid description of a piece of brain surgery he had witnessed that day to his wistful hope that professional people working with brain-injured patients would come to realize that the problem was in the brain, not in the peripheral symptoms of brain injury (such as paralysis, speech and learning problems).

That high-decibel conversation with Glenn remains clearly etched in my memory. His words kindled a raging curiosity. The fire still crackles today, fed over swiftly-passing years by uninterrupted replenishment of intensely combustible fuel.

"Please come visit," Glenn urged.

I assured him I would, then drove home with my wife. I babbled animatedly all the way, my mind aflame with exciting notions about the human brain and its potential. Floss seemed pleased. She knew how terribly bored I had always been at organizational dinners. She wasn't even remotely aware of how portentous this dinner had been. Nor was I.

In those days, I was a television newscaster, TV education editor, and proprietor of my own film production company. These vocations provided sufficient income and intellectual stimulation to keep me reasonably content. We owned our own home, were raising two splendid children: a baseball fan of ten, and an ebullient lass of six. The boat needed no rocking.

But rocking it got, and buffeting it still receives today, even as we approach the twenty-first century.

I responded to Glenn's enthusiastic invitation to visit. Not for just a brief couple of hours, rather, for repeated exposures to an entirely new dimension of life.

Back then, initial orientation lectures to parents of brain-injured children lasted about fifteen hours: Saturday all day through to wee hours on Sunday morning. With passing years, experience and mounting knowledge convinced the staff that a child's chance for normality improved the more his parents knew and understood. The introductory program grew to five very full days.

I couldn't stay away. Every spare minute found me returning. One day I found myself explaining to my wife that I really wasn't neglecting my film business; rather, my constant visits to Glenn Doman and his staff raised the possibility that a story about dealing *directly* with the brain instead of the peripheral symptoms of brain injury would make a fascinating documentary film.

Suddenly, I realized my excuse was quite accurate, and the flash of insight kindled a desire to write a motion picture scenario. But to develop a story that would make sense, I would have to learn more about the subject. Naturally, that was my business.

Doing research for other films had provided generous experience in all kinds of areas, but nothing before touched upon the brain. Industrial subjects involved manufacture of steel swimming pools, heating systems, multi-colored spray paint, toys and tank trucks; educational documentaries brought to the screen a tuberculosis sanatarium, a hobby association and a denture manufacturer. Each topic intrigued me for a time; then a new interest would woo me with the promise of intellectual stimulation and a modest profit.

An expanding world opened up, a world of receding horizon upon receding horizon. It wrenched outlook from the dream world of psychology to the reality of physiology. I learned that man's actions were not the result of an amorphous "mind"; they were, instead, the end product of a tangible brain. I read shelves of books about the brain, and completed The Institutes' course for nurses three times.

Glenn Doman explained how the brain of each well human being evolves at a stupendous, but ever-descending rate, from the moment of conception until six years of age. Principally, environmental factors determine the rate of maturation.

He stated simply that brain injury is rooted in the *brain*, not in the various affected parts of the body. He also asserted that the brain had an enormous untapped reserve. From this way of looking at the brain's potential, and of seeking ways to unleash it, he and his team had developed a rationale, procedures stemming from that rationale, methods and techniques for dealing directly with the brain, for helping children and adults reach ever-higher levels of performance.

I was hooked.

In 1961, we produced a film based on an article written by Institutes' staff and published by the *Journal of the American Medical Association*, September 17, 1960. The movie retained the title of the *Journal* article: "Children With Severe Brain Injuries: Neurological Organization in Terms of Mobility." It was released nearly four years after my initial meeting with Glenn.

During those four years my film business managed to hold its own. Television announcing was giving way to writing and producing videotape documentaries for WFIL-TV, Channel Six in Philadelphia. Time's flight quickened.

During Memorial Day weekend, 1962, I was enjoying a family barbecue when a phone call from Glenn summoned me to a meeting of "the greatest urgency." I had just been telling the family about a series of standardized reading tests we had administered to a little five-year-old child named Tommy Lunski. Tommy had been born brain-injured, his condition diagnosed, "very severe athetosis." At two, he was considered "incurable," and scheduled to spend a short life in an institution. Then he was brought to The Institutes by his parents. At five-years-of-age, after his family had worked with him intensively, Tommy was reading as well as a typical fifth grade pupil, *a child of eleven years*. He walked, talked, and was delightful in every way.

At the urgent meeting, Glenn announced we were going to examine carefully the question raised by Tommy's remarkable performance on the standardized reading tests; we were going to study the question, "If such a terribly brain-injured, very young child could learn to read, what was the matter with well older boys and girls who were having problems learning to read in school?"

We cited recent huge headlines lamenting the national reading scandal. Perhaps something in Tommy's reading ability held the clue to the strange paradox.

The staff met in uninterrupted session for three days and nights to ponder the matter. We munched sandwiches at what were approximate mealtimes, drank gallons of coffee, argued, and took time out only to go to the bathroom. Electrifying propositions set brains tingling. We were on to something big.

We knew that for thousands of years men of great wisdom had suspected human beings of functioning at only a few percent of their true potential. What that potential was remained unknown, perhaps never to be measured accurately.

Tommy Lunski's performance topped a series of results that had begun to occur with regularity at The Institutes. Tommy's parents had carried out a program that launched him on the road to achieving his potential.

We believed that, given a chance to take advantage of the enormous growth possibilities of the human brain and nervous system early in life, average boys and girls would be able to achieve their birthright, an inherent potential incredibly higher than contemporary man could imagine.

Two elements in the formula were utterly indispensable: the earliness at which a development program could begin, and the enthusiastic dedication of the child's mother and father.

Glenn hammered out a bold Statement of Objectives. The Institutes committed itself to "the significant increase of the ability of all children to perform in the physical, intellectual, physiological and social realms." He related developmental lags to lags in the development of the central nervous system. He declared that the speed at which brain maturation takes place "varies widely from human being to human being." He cited the use of The Institutes' Profile in determining a child's neurological age. He asserted that:

> . . . this process of neurological maturation can be *slowed slightly* by certain factors which prevent good brain organization. This process can be *slowed considerably* by certain environmental deprivations which create neurological dysorganization. This process can be *halted completely* by brain injury.

Most significantly, Glenn affirmed that "the process of neurological maturation *can be speeded as well as delayed,* and that this speeding can be accomplished by certain simple procedures."

We had demonstrated that *"neurological maturation,* which was formerly considered a static and irrevocable fact is instead a *dynamic and ever-changing process."*

We had also demonstrated an inescapable truth: the vital importance of the early years. That insight, inspired by Glenn Doman's *How To Teach*

Your Baby To Read, supplied the theme of a television documentary film, *How Soon The First R?* which I produced for Channel Six in Philadelphia. *How Soon The First R?* addressed the question of when a child really should begin to learn to read.

I traveled with our television crew around the country to film interviews with noted educators. At the University of Chicago, William Fowler actively helped very young children at two-years-of-age, his daughter among them, learn to read. He was successful, and the kids adored it.

At Yale University, Omar K. Moore had just invented the "talking typewriter." In his "learning laboratory," two-year-old children playing with the gadget were learning to read, and they were having a ball.

Near the television station, in Wyndmoor, just across the county line from Philadelphia, Glenn Doman was instructing local parents how to teach their two- and three-year-old children to read. He gave us their names and addresses, and we filmed the kids in action. By that time, Glenn's procedures had been used with hundreds of preschool brain-injured children and their well brothers and sisters. In 1963, his article, "How To Teach Your Baby To Read," was featured in the *Ladies Home Journal.*

At the TV station and at The Institutes my interest in early learning flamed hotter than an atomic core. Fourteen years out of undergraduate school, I returned to the University of Pennsylvania where

I worked for a Ph.D. in early education. The doctoral study quite naturally concerned early reading. It took the form of a television series which drew upon Glenn Doman's *How To Teach Your Baby To Read*. The series, *Wordland Workshop,* consisted of 195 half-hour programs that started in September, 1966, and ran through June, 1967.

My purpose was to investigate the effectiveness of a television curriculum, along with parental home cooperation, in helping three-year-old children learn to read. An original concept, as doctoral theses are supposed to be, *Wordland Workshop* preceded *Sesame Street* by three years.

The thirty-nine-week series was beamed each weekday, Monday through Friday, to an experimental group of children in and around Philadelphia. The control group of boys and girls watched *Captain Kangaroo*, a very popular network children's program, telecast in Binghamton, New York. *Captain Kangaroo* had a large cast of characters and many features designed to introduce the young TV viewer to varied aspects of contemporary civilization. The richly budgeted program also provided a generous measure of general language experience. But, it did not show words.

To make sure we were studying three-year-old children who were significantly alike, we matched 162 Binghamton-area children with the Philadelphia kids. For purposes of matching, we used sixteen criteria: pretest reading performance, verbal ability, socioeconomic status, mother's educational level, father's educational level, chronological age, sex, number of siblings, nursery school attendance, health, number of TV programs usually witnessed, the child's interest in TV, the child's interest in home-conducted reinforcement activities, parental competence, the child's prior interest in written language, and the child's social competence.

There were the usual pre-tests and post-tests. At the end of the thirty-nine weeks, all of the children in the experimental group had learned to read to a significant degree.

Parents reported that the kids had happily watched *Wordland Workshop* and had cheerfully engaged in home-learning activities.

One child in the control group recognized words on the post-test. Her mother had bought Glenn Doman's *How To Teach Your Baby To Read* a short time before the end of the television experiment.

The TV series added to my accumulating knowledge about early reading and convinced me that early reading is important, but that it was only a splinter compared to the towering early-learning tree. As numerous as leaves on that tree, a multitude of questions swirled: "Why do people wait until the kid is six-years-old before teaching reading—why not earlier, while learning spoken language?"

I was eager to know what was happening at the dawn of the life. "What helps infants learn so much so quickly?" "How come some get to be more intelligent than others, so intelligent, in fact, they're called 'gifted'?"

Precisely those questions were addressed when, in January, 1982, Glenn Doman and Richard Norton wrote "The Gifted Child Fallacy" for *The Elementary School Journal* (January 1982). They concluded:

- The growth of intelligence and the rate at which children are capable of learning (taking in raw data) is nearly an inverse function of age;
- Every newborn child has a huge neurological potential which often remains largely untapped;
- Every child is capable of much higher levels of function than normally occur;
- Parents are by far the best source for tapping the neurological resources of their young children;
- The central nervous system grows in size and in capabilities through early use in a process which rapidly diminishes beyond age 6;
- Being "gifted" is primarily a product of the environment and, by current definition, is a level of intelligence which can easily be reached by nearly every child.

The idea that all human beings are capable of becoming "gifted" excited me. I wanted to spend the rest of my life learning why it was possible and how to do it.

The moment my curiosity reached fever pitch, Glenn asked me to join the international team of Child-Brain Developmentalists at The Institutes for the Achievement of Human Potential.

I leapt to the challenge.

2

The Institutes

Whether Socrates had as high an I.Q. as Shakespeare or Descartes, Schweitzer or Einstein, will never be known. What is certain is that all such men used their brains as energetically as they knew how. Today, man may have no greater brain capacity than the ancients, but he has revolutionary ideas about how to exploit it.

This is the aim of neurologists, educators, and other researchers who are now organizing a group of Institutes for the Achievement of Human Potential. If they succeed, they will produce the Bacons of the 20th century—equally at home in computer theory and the kitchen garden, in the nucleus of the atom and all recorded literature.

TIME Magazine, January 11, 1963

Jay Cooke, who bore the same name as his grandfather, the famous financier who built the railroad that tied together both coasts of the United States, was a member of the Board of Directors when The Institutes was born. He described the mission of The Institutes in these words:

I view The Institutes for the Achievement of

Human Potential as an incredibly important teachers college.

He didn't mean that our faculty would prepare instructors for the public and private schools of the land. He meant that, as a nonprofit, tax-exempt organization in the highest category, we would show mothers how to help their children reach ever-higher levels of their innate potential.

The Institutes fulfills two principal responsibilities: Teaching parents how to make brain-injured children well, and teaching them how to make tiny well children "weller."

Our objective is to enable all children everywhere, both brain-injured and unhurt, to achieve their fullest potential in the following four areas: physical, physiological, intellectual, and social.

The way we do that is by teaching *parents* to help their children attain excellence in these four areas. We are convinced that parents are the best therapists and the best teachers in the world *if* they know what to do.

That truism became obvious only after the professional team of The Institutes for the Achievement of Human Potential began to help brain-injured kids gain improved function back in the forties, after World War II. Our research efforts throughout the ensuing years might best be described as "clinical investigation," a pragmatic activity that embraces successful theoretical models and practical therapy, and abandons conventional practices that don't work. Driving our search was the desire to find ways to get to the brain, the site of the problems our patients suffered, and make it function more efficiently.

From the beginning, our team, headed by Glenn Doman, proposed to treat the brain *directly,* instead of dealing with the peripheral symptoms of brain injury, such as paralysis, blindness, seizures, mental retardation, etc. In his lectures to parents, Glenn cites anatomy texts, dating from around the turn of the century, which emphasize that "central nervous system transmission can be accelerated by providing sensory stimulation with increased frequency, intensity, and duration." The only thing is, he points out, that particular piece of important information has been neglected over the years, for a number of reasons.

Not the least of these reasons is probably the amount of time required to carry out a program designed to teach a child's unused or underused brain cells to take over the responsibilities of cells killed or injured by some kind of a problem before or after birth, usually involving a shortage of oxygen. Depending on the severity of the brain injury, that amount of time can get to be quite demanding, sometimes all day, every day, seven days a week. For professional persons to teach the brain so that the child might see better, hear better, learn better, walk better, or talk better, the number of hours needed would command recompense well beyond what a modest middle-class budget could handle.

And while most professional people are kindly and love kids, they can no more match the love of parents for their own children than a fine saddle pony can win the Kentucky Derby.

We realized early on that parents could save huge amounts of their hard-earned money if they themselves carried out a carefully devised rehabilitation program, instead of relying on highly-paid professional people to do it. Parents were intelligent; they loved their kids; they would do anything to make them well.

We decided to teach parents what we had learned from our practical research. By the nineties, we had derived knowledge from intimate contact with more than thirty thousand parents and their fifteen thousand brain-injured children. After we learned how to apply that knowledge—modified, of course, to tiny well children—we taught another five thousand parents of healthy youngsters, ranging in age from birth to four years. Glenn Doman details this quest for answers in *What to Do About Your Brain-Injured Child*.

This knowledge and experience form the courses that, for the past forty years, we have been presenting to parents who travel to The Institutes in Chestnut Hill, just across the county line from Philadelphia, Pennsylvania. They come from one hundred seven countries on all six continents. They come to learn how to help their children reach ever-higher levels of their potential.

We have learned that to help both kinds of

children, *parents* are the answer. Parents are the best therapists in the world for their hurt children; parents are the best teachers in the world for their tiny well children. If . . .

That "if" is important.

May I repeat? Parents are the best therapists and the best teachers *if* they know what to do. And it's our job to teach them what to do.

WHAT HAPPENS AT THE INSTITUTES

Four Institutes work directly with parents and their children. The staffs of these Institutes teach parents how to help their brain-injured children become well, and their well children reach higher levels of function.

Three of these four Institutes concentrate on helping brain-injured children. They are The Institute for the Achievement of Physiological Excellence, the Institute for the Achievement of Physical Excellence, and The Institute for the Achievement of Intellectual Excellence.

Child-brain developmentalists and physicians of The Institute for the Achievement of Physiological Excellence evaluate brain-injured children who are blind, deaf, and insensate. They design specific functional neurological programs, and teach parents how to help such children come to see, hear, and feel. They evaluate brain-injured children who suffer epileptic seizures, design specific functional neurological programs, and teach parents how to eliminate the convulsions. They evaluate brain-injured children who suffer multiple, often life-threatening, medical problems, design specific functional programs, and teach parents how to help such children to enjoy robust health.

Long years ago, back in September 1960, *The Journal of the American Medical Association* published the initial report of The Institutes' functional neurological organization program. The patterning program was described at length. The article graphically illustrated how patterners simulate movements of crawling and creeping by moving a patient's arms and legs, thereby superimposing the tactile stimulation of those movements on the central nervous system.

This seminal *Journal* article also mentioned The Institutes' "masking" program by which the patient is enabled to breathe his own exhaled carbon dioxide. A little plastic mask, the kind used in hospitals to provide oxygen support, is placed over a patient's nose frequently and for varying duration a specific number of times during the day. This procedure takes advantage of the fact that carbon dioxide is the world's most potent vasodilator. A little cluster of cell bodies sits at the juncture of the carotid arteries heading toward the brain. These cell bodies detect the amount of carbon dioxide in the blood. When the optimum level is exceeded, the blood vessels dilate. After the mask is removed, and for an extended period of time, the patient benefits from an increased flow of oxygen-rich blood, along with nutrients and vital trace elements, to the brain.

The child-brain developmentalists of The Institute for the Achievement of Physical Excellence evaluate brain-injured children who range from those who are completely paralyzed, through children who have incapacitating mobility problems, to children who are poorly coordinated. These specialists help design specific functional neurological programs, and teach parents how to help such children to crawl, creep, walk, run, and perform gymnastic routines.

The child-brain developmentalists of The Institute for the Achievement of Intellectual Excellence evaluate brain-injured children who appear to lack all understanding, who are mute, unable to learn, or unable to learn to read or write or compute. They design specific functional neurological programs, and teach parents how to help such children come to speak, to learn, to learn to read, and often to surpass their peers in intellectual performance.

The fourth of The Institutes that work directly with parents and children is The Evan Thomas Institute for Early Development. The staff of this Institute (the same team of child-brain developmentalists who work with parents of brain-injured children) teaches parents how to help their tiny well children reach ever-higher levels of function.

To do this, they conduct the How to Multiply Your Baby's Intelligence course, a seven-day program presented several times each year to parents who want to help their babies and very young children benefit from the magic early years. (See Appendix B.)

While children remain at home in the loving care of grandparents or relatives, mothers and fathers attend a minimum of eight hours of lectures and demonstrations each day. They also profit from numerous ten-minute "coffee breaks" during which they pose questions to the staff. They learn *why* they should help their tiny children to learn how to read and to do math, to become physically superb, to become socially adept, to learn foreign languages, and to play the violin. They also learn *how* to accomplish all this. Participants of this course who may, themselves, not be able to do gymnastics or speak a foreign language, learn procedures, methods, and techniques that help them to help very young children acquire these abilities.

The Evan Thomas Institute for Early Development also presents the Off-Campus Early Development Program. Parents who have successfully completed the How to Multiply Your Baby's Intelligence course are eligible to receive ongoing instruction. For example, off-campus participants may confer with staff each week on the telephone and, each month, receive a packet of Institutes' early-learning materials.

The faculty of the Evan Thomas Institute for Early Development is comprised of nine teachers who have been certified by the Commonwealth of

Pennsylvania. They conduct The International School, licensed by the state as a private academic school for young children.

The International School is a demonstration school. In many ways it is a prototype, a model to be emulated by all schools everywhere. Because it is a demonstration school, where parents work side-by-side with child-brain developmentalists, and where children participate actively during the How to Multiply Your Baby's Intelligence course, all of the children are granted full scholarships.

The main objective of The International School is to enable Institutes' early-learning children to build upon their already considerable knowledge and skills.

Two service institutes contribute knowledge and train personnel for the practicing Institutes: The Edward LeWinn Institute for Search, Research and Clinical Innovation, and The Temple Fay Institute for Academics.

The Edward LeWinn Institute for Search, Research and Clinical Innovation devises and carries out practical clinical investigation projects. For instance, when the progress of a brain-injured child toward wellness seems to "plateau," that child—an example of children who exhibit similar symptoms of brain-injury—often comes to The Institutes for intensive study by the entire staff. The child and his parents remain as Institutes' guests until a key is found to insure continuing progress.

Among significant contributions of The Edward

LeWinn Institute for Search, Research and Clinical Innovation are: the use of the mask for re-breathing one's own carbon dioxide; the overhead ladder for helping brain-injured children learn to walk; and perhaps most important, the mobility and respiratory patterning programs.

The Temple Fay Institute for Academics is the teaching arm of The Institutes. It organizes and presents courses at the undergraduate and graduate levels for parents and professionals, and recognizes successful completion of those courses with appropriate certification.

For graduate students, The Temple Fay Institute offers programs in child-brain development: at the developmentalist level, the teaching level, and the preceptor level. Curriculum content is approved by the International Academy for Child-Brain Development. The graduate courses are designed for professional people from all over the world who wish to become child-brain developmentalists. Candidates have earned their undergraduate and graduate degrees, come from many medical specialties and therapies, and from anthropology and education.

Upon successful completion of their course, they are board certified by the International Academy for Child-Brain Development. They are then also eligible to become members of The Institutes international staff, women and men who have resolved to teach parents how to raise a generation of highly capable children, human beings who come ever-closer to reaching their potential.

RESULTS OF THE INSTITUTES' EARLY-LEARNING PROGRAM

Seeing thousands upon thousands of brain-injured children on an intimate basis, teaching their mothers and fathers how to help them overcome agonizing problems, intensively studying more thousands of well brothers and sisters of hurt kids: this hard-nosed experience day in and day out for many decades taught our staff how tiny human beings are supposed to grow and develop.

We learned about well kids by helping brain-injured children become well.

Just over thirty years ago, we began teaching parents to teach their babies to read at ages from birth to four years. Then, as tales of success began to reach us, programs were rapidly developed for aiding parents to teach tiny children math, Bits of Intelligence (covering a range as wide as that of an encyclopedia) and problem-solving, to acquire social graces, to play the violin, and to become adept at gymnastics.

Glenn Doman's book, *How to Teach Your Baby to Read,* became a world-wide perennial best-seller. A cascade of letters in response to the book billowed into a torrent. Today, Glenn's files bulge with tens of thousands of reports from parents who enjoyed teaching their children to read and to learn much, much more.

The letters describe how those parents carried out The Institutes' early learning program in an atmosphere of joy and warmth and love. The writers, mostly mothers, emphasize that they taught their children to learn *how* to learn. The children established learning habits for the rest of their lives and now enjoyed an immense array of options. For instance, when the young ones had gained an insight into the language of mathematics, they saw math being used everywhere around them, on shopping trips, and in real-life math games and puzzles.

Stories arriving from many countries revealed an extraordinary diversity of customs, interests, and tastes. Each family had highlighted their own individual interests. The mountain of letters discloses that families who were attracted by nature welcomed their children into the captivating world of facts about plants and animals. Young children thrilled more to using the name "German shepherd" than "bow-wow" or "doggie." "Daisy" added a richer dimension to the child's burgeoning knowledge than "flower," and "monarch butterfly" added more substance to the child's vocabulary than "bug."

Science-minded parents introduced their very young children to chemistry, biology, and astronomy. Bits of information about minerals and cells and stars turned the physical world into an engrossing and mysterious wonderland.

History buffs fed their kids a rich bank of data concerning striking personalities and momentous events of the past. Curious and very human facts about United States presidents, historical art and musical figures made famous men and women come alive.

Parents, conscious of our ever-shrinking planet, our global village, provided their very young ones with an opportunity to learn another language in the earliest years when it's easiest to do so. The kids also achieved not only vocabulary, but also proper accent, rhythm, and music.

Other parents, aware of the danger to the planet, due to ignorance of the effects of human tampering with Earth's delicate balance, presented their children with generous opportunities to learn about rivers, mountains, and jungles. Early on, the children became accutely aware of the complexity of ecology.

Tiny children, aching to be like big boys and girls, became in every sense of the term, young research scholars. They begged to be taken to the library where they could seek information on their own. They shouted with glee when parents and friends gave them books on favorite subjects. They amassed a large and meaningful vocabulary. Their imagination and creativity soared. They expressed themselves with ease and originality.

These children visited zoos, museums, concerts, and theaters. They were being introduced early to the treasurehouse of human knowledge, at a time of life when their brains were soaking up everything like water into Sahara sands.

They ran and jumped and swam, and became splendid gymnasts. They learned ballet and acquired grace and coordination.

They learned table manners à la Emily Post. They

mastered and practiced common rules of courtesy: "Thank you," "Please," and "Excuse me." They saw their families observing the Golden Rule; they absorbed proper behavior and acted accordingly.

Parents related how their children were beginning to combine seemingly distinct pieces of knowledge in unique and interesting ways. Institutes' early-learning children were drawing upon great vaults of knowledge, seeking raw material with which to fashion original, creative, and often bold, solutions to problems. Self-assurance grew in proportion to the extent that young children became intellectually, physically, and socially capable. As these children reached five or six, school-entry age around the world, parents marveled.

Academically, children would be entering first-grade reading at an advanced level, speaking at least one other language besides their native tongue, and computing at either the junior-high school or high-school level.

Physically, children would be entering first grade already running three miles a day, swimming many lengths of an Olympic-sized swimming pool, and performing complicated gymnastic routines.

In music and the arts, children would be entering first grade already playing the violin or another musical instrument, drawing and painting, and writing stories.

Socially, children would be entering first grade already having mastered basic rules of courtesy, showing compassion for fellow human beings, and behaving properly at restaurants, theaters, and parties.

A very natural question began to crop up: "What's going to happen when my early learner goes to school?"

The day their kids must report to school arrives all too soon.

After what seems to have been a mere fleeting moment of great joy for both parents and tiny children, the child is ready to leave the protective warmth of the family cocoon. He climbs the tall front steps leading up to the imposing red brick building with the Grecian columns, tugs at, and finally opens the big wooden-and-glass front door, and enters a new world—the world of "school."

3

Early Learners
Go to School

For there is the realization coming home to every-
body that our educational system is deteriorating.
The remedy invoked by the Federal Government,
the NEA, State and Local boards–the spending of
billions of dollars–is clearly not a solution. The
more money we spend, the more the problem is
compounded. Not only are the students becoming
more illiterate, but now the teachers themselves are
showing themselves inept.

Dr. Robert Morris

D r. Morris' silvered glass sharply mirrors the
disease that afflicts schools these days, not only
in the United States, but in most nations. The favorite
medicine of the past, money, no longer seems to do
the trick, somewhat in the way certain antibiotics
become unable to cure a sick patient. The mutant bug
eating away at our educational system has become
resistant. Despite this distressing fact, at this writing,
federal, state and local governments spend more than
$262 billion annually on schools and colleges.

Nowhere near that kind of money was needed

when schools were first getting started a few hundred years ago. Back then, just a tiny number of children attended what might be termed a "school." Shakespeare did. He didn't like it very much. Remember:

> Then, the whining school-boy, with his satchel, and shining morning face, creeping like snail unwillingly to school.

Three hundred years later, in nineteenth-century America, big city buildings, rural "little red schoolhouses"—with one room and a pot-bellied stove—and tiny private "Academies" turned out sufficient numbers of citizens to get our fledgling republic started and on its way.

During that last century, and for a number of years during the early decades of this one, kids were needed to help out with chores on the farm. In the country and in cities, children fortunate enough to be born into families where "book-larnin'" was respected, learned to read at about the same time they learned to understand spoken language. The father of America's eminent essayist and philosopher, Ralph Waldo Emerson, complained to a friend, "Little Ralph has just turned three, and he's having some problems with his Bible reading." At that time, of course, most of young America's population didn't enjoy little Ralph's cultured background, and the largest percentage of citizens remained illiterate.

In the hundred years since Emerson's time, a shattering population explosion teamed up with great floods of immigrants pouring in from around the world. If the United States were to be a democracy, the new generation of children had to be educated. The vitality of this brave new democracy depended on the quality of instruction they would receive.

With fathers out manning factories and cultivating fields; with mothers home cooking, cleaning, mending, giving birth and minding toddlers; young children of six and seven, who had reached "the age of reason" attended school. Our citizenry, multinational and rainbow-colored; our educators, conservative, moderate, and radical; our teachers, caring and bright, dull and insensitive—all were obliged to be profoundly dedicated to public education.

The challenge was then, and still is today, daunting.

In that early time, great religious institutions, ever-mindful of the power of education, founded the first schools. Secular demands quickly changed the complexion of the curriculum. In the present era, in the United States, 15,747 independent public school districts determine and execute their own individual educational programs.

The school boards, all 15,747 of them, set policies, determine curricula and hire teachers. These boards, popularly-elected, reflect the sentiments of the people in their individual communities. They, and an additional 28,734 private and parochial schools, are at liberty to teach pretty much what and how they please.

These are the schools our kids, who had engaged in The Institutes' early-development program with their parents, go to when they reach compulsory education age. The first step of their preparation began when their parents attended The Institutes' course that bears the same name as Glenn Doman's book, *How To Multiply Your Baby's Intelligence.*

In Chapter One of the first edition of that book Glenn describes a typical class:

> They are parents, every last one of them, excepting only the four who are about to be, and being parents they ask all the right questions, the ones to which they had come so far to find answers. They ask all the positive questions which their instinctual behavior as parents and their natural hope as parents who love their children very much causes them to ask.
>
> Is it possible to improve my baby's abilities? Can I make him a brighter, healthier, more capable, more loving, happier, more creative child than he would otherwise be or are his characteristics born into him and basically unchangeable? If I can make him more effective, as I strongly suspect I can, how do I do it?
>
> Being human beings, they also ask all the negative questions that their fears and programming of long-standing myths, together with much professional bullying, had drummed into them.
>
> "If I can improve my child's abilities and even

his intelligence so that he becomes above average, won't that be a bad thing for him? If he is better than the other kids, won't he be a misfit and disliked? If I teach him to read and write and do math at only one year of age, won't he be bored when he gets to school? . . ."

Much evidence appearing throughout Glenn's mountain of letters, from parents who had read his books and put his recommendations into practice while children were in their preschool years, demonstrated powerfully that only good things happened after those early learners had entered school. Yet, somehow, the question continued to be raised.

It came up again as we approached the decade of the nineties. It was mentioned during our critique, the customary daily session we hold at the end of each course day. We were all seated around a large oval table. Each developmentalist, in turn, described encounters with parents during ten-minute break periods between fifty-minute lectures. We discussed questions raised, questions such as whether everyone understood the vitally important *why,* and whether participants were enjoying the demonstrations. We asked ourselves, "How can we make the course better next time?"

That's when the question about what would happen when the child entered school was raised again. We wanted to give an exact answer.

We suddenly realized that more than a decade had sped by since the first How To Multiply Your

Baby's Intelligence course. Many children who had engaged in The Institutes' early-learning program between birth and four-years-of-age way back then were now attending school.

Parents and teachers could now tell us what actually happened when those children entered school.

We resolved to discover the exact answer to what happens to Institutes' early learners when they go to school. No longer would we depend solely upon our firm conviction that only positive things would happen. Inasmuch as all staff developmentalists were deeply involved all day, every day, with parents and children, logically, the task of finding the answer fell to me.

THE SURVEY

We wanted to learn what happened to those kids whose parents had carried out an Institutes' early-learning program before they went to school.

They were children whose parents had helped them acquire many abilities important once they entered school. They began school with abilities like knowing how to read, to compute, to be able to participate successfully in physical activities.

To obtain information about school performance and behavior, we would not have to contact every single parent of the thousands who had come to The Institutes.

Many hundreds of those families had kept in

touch. Some had attended the How To Multiply Your Baby's Intelligence course and had gone home and created an enhanced learning environment for their tiny children. Others had joined the Off-Campus Program and had received ongoing assistance from the Institutes' staff. These parents were our "target population." All we had to do was to select at random a significantly large number who had carried out an Institutes' early learning program.

To do that, we asked the computer to select, at random, candidates for the survey, and it provided names of 350 families whose children were now attending school.

We prepared a questionnaire that contained the following key questions:

- "What is your child's present age?"
- "What is your child's present grade in school?"
- "How is your child doing intellectually? Specifically, in reading and math?"
- "How is your child doing physically? Specifically, in gym and in schoolyard games?"
- "How is your child doing socially? Specifically, what are relations like with peers, teachers, other adults?"

The grades of the children were as varied as their ages, although some of the children were "ungraded." Ungraded simply means that these children were being home-taught, or were currently enrolled in school programs modelled after the one-room schoolhouses of the nineteenth century. These children are not graded because they are enabled to work at their highest level, often being tutored by the older children.

The scoring system posed a wee bit of a problem.

In the United States, all of those 15,747 independent public school districts we mentioned earlier (some districts containing many schools), and the 28,734 private and parochial schools are at liberty to use whatever kind of scoring system they choose. This includes a bewildering array, ranging from digits and decimals—1.50, 2.00, 3.9, 4.00—to letters—A, B, C, D, E, F—to marking on a sophisticated Gaussian curve.

We chose the most direct, easily understood, method: "Excellent, Good, Fair, and Poor."

We also asked parents to describe their feelings about having engaged in The Institutes' early learning program. We encouraged them to discuss at length what actually happened when their Institutes' early learner went to school.

The questionnaires were dispatched and, within weeks, we tabulated the following return:

GENERAL QUESTIONNAIRE RESPONSE

- Number of questionnaires mailed: 350
- Returned by post-office, undeliverable: 42

- Number of families receiving questionnaires: 308
- Not returned: 69
- Number of families returning questionnaires: 239
- Percentage of return from families to whom questionnaires were delivered: 78%
- Number of children about whom information was provided: 314
- Number of boys: 170
- Number of girls: 144

Of the surveyed Institutes' early-learners, 273 (87 percent) were attending either public or private schools, the remaining 41 (13 percent) were being home-schooled.

What had we expected in terms of response to this survey? We were optimistic, of course, that the survey would be successful, because we knew the parents; they had read the books, attended the course, and carried out a superb off-campus program in accordance with what they had learned.

We were hoping that not too many parents would have moved away. It's no secret that we have probably one of the most mobile populations of any nation on earth and, therefore, we were delighted that so many did reply to the questionnaires, did let us know how their children had fared once they had gone to school.

Table 3.1 Breakdown of Children's Ages in the Survey

Present Age	Number of Children	Present Age	Number of Children
6	2	15	8
7	3	16	13
8	5	17	8
9	48	18	10
10	41	19	5
11	64	20	4
12	36	21	1
13	33	23	2
14	31		
		Total Children 314	

Table 3.2 School Grade Breakdown of Early-Learning Children

Present Grade	Number of Children	Present Grade	Number of Children
1	2	8	18
2	3	9	12
3	5	10	4
4	35	11	7
5	41	12	7
6	40	College	3
7	19	Ungraded	118
		Total Children 314	

Our confidence that the children would be doing well was also built upon the very firm foundation of first-hand evidence; we already knew what was happening to the children who lived in the vicinity of The Institutes. Their parents were just like other parents whose names popped up on the computer print-out. As it happened, a number of the children were attending The Evan Thomas Institute for Early Development. We had daily contact with these kids and their parents. The nine certified teachers on our staff provided weekly reports of progress. And that progress thrilled us.

Concerning the astonishingly large percentage of replies we received from parents all over the nation and the world, after such a long period of time, we were not really surprised. Nor did the tremendous accomplishments of their children bowl us over. After all, we had been receiving update letters for a decade.

What we wanted to do, and what we believe has been accomplished, was to gather sufficient data so that we might share our delight, and perhaps inspire other parents also to engage in a marvelously joyful and salutary early development program with their babies, infants, toddlers, three-, four-, and five-year-old children.

Now, let's consider the results.

4

The Survey Results

For ten years, the German Sports Academy, Cologne, conducted scientific tests to determine the effects of early swimming on later performance in life.

Three groups of children were tested: the first started swimming at 2 months, the second when they were 2 years old; and the third group was given no swimming instructions at all but were used as a control group.

Parents and trainers observed that as the 2-month-old infants grew up, they showed more independence, reliance, confidence, and intelligence in decision-making than other children their own age.

West German Health Ministry, 1979

If we were little kids, and we were in school, much of how we felt about ourselves would come from how we were doing in reading and math and the other school subjects. If we did well, we would feel great; if we did only average work, many factors would come into play about how we would feel about ourselves; factors like, "What are mom and dad gonna say about it?" and later on, "Will I be able to get into the kind of college that will help me succeed in life?" Or even, "Will I be able to get a job?"

Relative to such questions, it's clear that, in general terms, school measurements were most encouraging for our surveyed kids who are currently attending school in thirty-four states and twelve countries. Overall, the measures indicated that the children, having come to school well-acquainted with the written word and the basic processes of computing, do startlingly better than their classmates who didn't enjoy similar opportunities in their preschool years. From the survey responses we learned that:

- 214 Institutes' early-learners learned to read at ages far below the ages they would have normally been taught.

- 142 Institutes' early-learners had learned to do math at ages far below the ages they would normally be taught.

- 52 Institutes' early-learners had learned at least one other language beside their own more than a dozen years before they might have had the opportunity to do so in school.

- 127 Institutes' early-learners had assimilated knowledge as broad and as filled with facts as the world around them, such as names and facts concerning: famous historical figures, sea life, geography, geology, music, evolution, physiology, biology, philosophy, art, mathematics, astronomy, chemistry, transportation, literature, and language.

The program benefited the children in other aspects, as well. Parents' open-ended comments revealed that the little kids in our Institutes' survey had enjoyed heightened physical and aerobic activities of every kind during preschool years.

They ran outdoors to heart's content. They swam as if the pool had no boundaries. They danced and performed gymnastic routines, never wanted to stop, and sailed through an entire spectrum of joyful physical programs, activities catalogued by parents in our survey (See Table 4.1).

The surveyed children had musical talents as varied as their physical talents. Most of the surveyed children learned how to play the violin and other instruments via the Suzuki method. 148 of these children had learned to play at least one musical instrument before entering elementary school (see Table 4.2). The violin was the most popular choice; the piano, the second.

All of the school children in the survey were judged on how well they performed socially, intellectually, and physically. Judgment depended upon a welter of grading systems. Still, one notices that, in one form or another, "A, B, C, D," or, "Satisfactory +, Satisfactory, Satisfactory -, Unsatisfactory, " all of the methods boil down to the old-fashioned "Excellent, Good, Fair," and, heaven forbid, "Poor."

**Table 4.1 A Breakdown of the Athletic Interests
of the Children in the Survey**

Question: "List your child's physical accomplishments before entering
school. (Running, swimming, gymnastics, etc.)"

Physical Activity	Number of Children	Physical Activity	Number of Children
Swimming	223	Soccer	6
Gymnastics	97	Diving	4
Running	86	Ice Skating	4
Ballet/Dance	32	Karate	4
Biking	19	Judo	3
Roller Skating	11	Taekwondo	2
Skiing	9	Trampoline	2
Hiking	8	Baseball	1
Horseback Riding	8	Basketball	1
Tennis	8	Climbing	1

This was the most widely-used scoring system. To determine what had happened in reading and math to the children who had followed an early learning program once they reached school, parents were asked to score their early-learning children using this easily-understood system: "E, G, F, P." Parents were to use their own judgment, combined with comments on official school report cards and teacher observations, and come up with an evaluation of their child's ability.

Most of the surveyed parents specified *exactly* how their kids should be rated. A small minority of the parents, those who were home-schooling their kids who had no official reports to go by, and those in schools using the "Pass/Fail" grading system, did not provide any scores.

**Table 4.2 A Breakdown of the Musical Interests
of the Children in the Survey**

Instrument	Number of Children	Instrument	Number of Children
Violin	82	Flute	2
Piano	53	Organ	2
Cello	4	Accordion	1
Harp	3	Xylophone	1
		Total	148

SOCIALLY SPEAKING

Naturally parents were pleased when their child came home from school with all "A's"; they were delighted when their child excelled in gymnastics, swimming and various sports activities. But, it became increasingly clear that, in response to the question, "What happened to your child when he got to school?" they were happiest when they reported how the youngster got along with classmates.

INTELLECTUALLY SPEAKING

Many of the surveyed parents admitted they had wanted their children to excel, meaning they wanted their children to do better than average children do once they had entered school and gone out into life. But, emphatically, their main motivation was not to lord it over their neighbors, nor to be prouder than all parents naturally are about their childrens' accomplishments. The

Table 4.3 The Social Behavior of the
Children in the Survey

Question: "How is your child doing socially? Specifically, how are relations with peers, teachers, other adults?"

	Excellent	Good	Fair	Poor
Responses	221	61	14	1
Percentages	74%	21%	5%	0.3%

parents who had engaged in the early development program simply wanted to insure that their kids were equipped in a superior way to meet life's difficulties. They wanted their sons and daughters to have copious options in life to make and to find for themselves happiness and fulfillment.

PHYSICALLY SPEAKING

Even the ancients knew about the value of exercise. Back in the very first century of the present era, the famous Roman poet, Juvenal, wrote: *Mens sana in corpore sana,* which means "A sound mind in a sound body." Back then, in the year 75 A.D., Juvenal came to his conclusions by studying the people around him. He noticed that those acquaintances of his who were physically in good shape were, in general, sharp, witty, and bright.

The philosopher John Locke did the same thing. After keenly observing the people he knew, Locke asserted, "A sound mind in a sound body is a short but full description of a happy state in this world."

**Table 4.4 The Intellectual Capabilities of the
Children in the Survey: Reading**

Question: "How is your child doing intellectually? (a) In reading?"

	Excellent	Good	Fair	Poor
Responses	254	31	3	1
Percentages	88%	10%	0.1%	0.03%

**Table 4.5 The Intellectual Capabilities of the
Children in the Survey: Math**

Question: "How is your child doing intellectually? (b) In math?"

	Excellent	Good	Fair	Poor
Responses	227	55	9	2
Percentages	77%	19%	3%	1%

Neither Juvenal nor Locke had to wait until jogging became popular in the mid-sixties of the present century before they came to their conclusions. They didn't have to wait for bicycles to crowd mountain trails. Nor did they have to wait for the famous Harvard study of some 3,500 graduates which most convincingly established that vigorous exercise was one of the most important factors contributing to a longer, healthier, happier, more productive life.

REAL PREPARATION FOR SCHOOL

Parents of early learners almost universally describe their children as "school proof."

What exactly is being "school proof?" In a very

**Table 4.6 How Parents Rated Their
Early Learners Physically**

Question: "How is your child doing physically? Specifically, in gym and
in schoolyard games?"

	Excellent	Good	Fair	Poor
Responses	195	85	13	2
Percentages	66%	29%	4%	1%

real sense, it's a condition much like being "fire proof," "water proof," or "weather proof." One may assume that the substance described, "fire," "water," or "weather," is threatening an object, and by the application of a protective substance, the material is provided with the strength to resist. By providing children with the protective substance of knowledge, parents are giving their children the strength to endure our weak school system.

Here, we need not dwell overlong on the abysmal state that most schools currently find themselves in; the press is doing a yeoman's job with that assignment. All we need to do is mention that, by the time the surveyed children reached school, they had been the lucky recipients of programs designed to take advantage of their fantastic learning powers while they were very young. Their parents, like architects drawing plans for an ideal home, anticipated the daunting challenges the kids would face in every direction once they entered school.

Since these mothers and fathers had no crystal ball, they did the best they could. They tried to provide background experiences and information that would give the kids the widest number of options later on. They called upon their own knowledge and savvy in certain fields; asked relatives, friends, and neighbors to help out with their areas of expertise; hunted up tons of data from a vast variety of sources—literature, poetry, nature books, botanical and zoological gardens, atlases, history texts, art collections, museums, sporting events, orchestra performances, and encyclopedias.

During those preschool learning sessions, when their kids showed more than a glimmer of interest in a particular area, parents fed that interest. When their children were not intrigued by a specific subject, they postponed or entirely dropped it. They refined talent; they fired imagination; they equipped their children with experiences of the real and practical world against the day the kids would enter school.

These early-leaners—well-rounded, with a load of options under their belts—would be able to face most any challenge. They had benefited from an early-learning program par excellence. Underlying their early-learning program was the conviction that, if a very young child achieves intellectual excellence, physical excellence, and social excellence, he would become, by definition, competent.

The truism that competence usually breeds confidence is nowhere else more apparent than in school. And, conversely, it seems quite obvious that those children in a school setting who are insecure intellectually, physically, and socially are the ones who encounter, and create, problems in school. But a child entering school possessing high self-esteem, leadership qualities, respect and compassion for fellow human beings, a strong love of learning, a congenial personality, creativity, and mature judgment may justifiably be termed, "school proof."

Surveyed parents were mainly interested in finding schools that would harmonize with their kids' early learning. One dad, Arthur Streeter, from Texas, reported, "We searched for a school where classes were more advanced and more challenging."

In Westmont, New Jersey, Heather Lippincott and her mother "mutually decided to get the best out of what was available" in school and "enthusiastically expand on learning outside of school. If, however, my child had been a poor student, understanding might not have been so easily achieved." Heather's teachers have been enthusiastic and helpful, and her parents actively participate in all aspects of the small school's programs.

In the Northeastern United States, Alyssa Wolf, of Massachusetts, went directly into a school for the gifted where her teachers were keenly receptive to her needs. They tried hard to balance her "enormous intellectual capacity and drive for more and more knowledge" with spelling, phonics, structure, etc., and were sensitive to her needs.

Robbie Parry, of Framingham, Massachusetts, was far advanced academically and, having had the advantage of early learning, "has stayed on top in class."

In the Mid-Atlantic region, Amber Dolan, at the head of her class, "learns easily." She tolerates the annoyance of the slow and repetitious parts of the school program in order "to reap the benefits of the social aspect and the wide range of subjects they cover." Her mother reflects, "Amber got a great start in learning, and is staying a step above her classmates."

Nikki Darter lived in New York before moving to Florida. There she tested well and received a large scholarship to a private school. Now, in public school in her new State, she "is designated as gifted and is granted one day with an enrichment teacher and her third grade peers."

Another Florida early learner, Ernie Falco, attends a full-time gifted program in the public schools. His program, supervised by one teacher and many parent volunteers, benefits fifteen children. He's given "lots of challenging academics along with problem solving and thinking activities. They learn Spanish, become accomplished in art and music, work out in PE, and master the computer."

In Georgia, Virginia Brumby was totally exempted from all math for the second and third grades, and the public school let her move up for advanced language arts.

On the Pacific Coast, at the Los Angeles United

School Magnet for the gifted/high achieving, Riley Sorrells' teacher admits freely that "he is one of the brightest children in class. You can ask or quiz him on any of the work covered and he knows it all 100%, and can elaborate on his answers."

In Simi Valley, California, Tucker Ross' parents found a school that "accelerates all children in accordance with their knowledge and abilities."

Still on the West Coast, by the time she reached school, Institutes' early learner Alayna Thompson had learned "thousands of Bits, words, books, and subjects." When she entered kindergarten, she was tested by the school system, and one month after her fifth birthday, three months into the fourth grade, she was assessed at the level of a ten-year-old child, a 4.3 level.

In Arizona, Jill Peterson was placed in her school's gifted program and is accelerated in math and reading. She also participates in the Arizona State University Center for Academic Superiority.

Over in Texas, James Williams has an excellent teacher and thoroughly enjoys the social interaction and projects. He has access to fifteen IBM PC computers, one per child. James and his classmates are allowed to work at their own pace. He "gets a big kick out of being creative and writing his own stories."

In Colorado, Jill Conklin, of Longmont, had entered an advanced reading program and in nearby Utah, Christian Mansfield "was admitted to ELP, a program for very advanced children where he is flourishing."

Parents of the 41 children being home-schooled sent the following information about their children:

Kevin Hawkins, of Escondido, California, is enrolled in a unique Alternative School Program offered through the Ramona Unified School District. Kevin is not required to attend classes; he can go as seldom or as often as he likes. He completes contracts mailed to his teacher and is tested twice a year. At home, he follows basic school courses supplemented by violin lessons, Japanese and gymnastics. He is also on the Escondido swim team.

Eight van Arragon children, ages seven to seventeen, attend their mom's home school in Canada. As Institutes' early learners, they start at birth with a rich program of stimulation. They begin reading by age one and rapidly gain speed, fluency, and comprehension. The kids acquire encyclopedic knowledge with the aid of Bits of Intelligence and they receive exposure to half-a-dozen languages. At the same time, they're trained in a variety of practical skills.

At twelve or thirteen, the van Arragon children enter high school where they readily adapt and adjust to the demands of formal schooling. They appear to be "immune to the tyranny of the peer group, the necessity of adolescent rebellion, and other fads and fashions."

When she was seventeen, Judy van Arragon spent seven weeks in Taiwan, where she studied

Mandarin, Chinese history, and calligraphy, among other things. Mom and Dad travel widely with the children, and "enjoy touring the great museums, art galleries, and other cultural institutions." Their children are fully involved in family hobbies and pastimes. According to their parents they develop an active interest in such diverse avocations as "gardening, canoeing, hunting, and piano tuning and repairs."

Like the van Arragon brood, early learner Josh Pereira was home-schooled since babyhood. Now, having graduated from The Institutes' Evan Thomas International School, he relates:

> *When I was fourteen, I spent two months in a regular high school. I entered at the ninth grade because everyone else in that class was either 14 or 15. They were studying Algebra One, which is basic algebra. They had problems like "3X + 6 = 5X. Solve for X." I had finished that type of algebra two years before, so I passed every test 100%. In the English class, the assignment was to read "Never Cry Wolf" by Farley Mowat. It was a paperback with about 180 pages. The assignment was to read five pages a night and write a short half-page essay on those five pages and bring it in the next day. Then, in class they would discuss the Chapter titles before the class had read them and try to guess what the chapter might be about.*
>
> *I read the whole book the first night, by accident. I had intended to follow the directions of the homework, but the book was so interesting I couldn't put*

it down. (I've reread it 5 times since then.) In school the next day, the other kids had read two pages, one page, zero pages.

Everyone groaned when the teacher gave ten pages for homework that night. One person was certain that the eyestrain involved with reading ten pages would blind him before he was 20. When I mentioned to the teacher that I had finished the book, and had handed him a four-page book report the morning after the assignment, he decided to give me two books for homework: "The Animal Farm" and "Marigolds." I read them both that night and wrote the reports the next two days in class.

For the rest of the time I was in that school, I wrote for the school newspaper.

Overseas, Stevie Conner, at five years of age, entered a Scottish school. He was far ahead of his peers; his reading age was that of a twelve-year-old child. He still expressed his "rage to learn." In Great Britain parents have the option to teach kids at home, a choice Stevie's parents made. "The authorities sighed with relief."

At the age of eight and a half, when his parents felt he "was mature enough to cope with insensitive teaching methods, he marched off to school. He adapted well to peers, and was very sociable." The parents moved to France to give his language skills a boost. Now, in French school, Stevie is "happy and fluent, and intriguing them with his inventions."

"SOMETHING STRANGE IS HAPPENING. . . "

In March, 1984, Rod McLeish, in the *Smithsonian Magazine*, spoke of "giftedness:"

> There is some evidence that the nation's population of gifted children—and, possibly, prodigies—is growing. James T. Webb, professor and assistant dean at Wright State University in Dayton, Ohio, reports that staff members at the institution who test large numbers of children have detected a startling proportion in the 170-to-180 IQ range. "Something strange is happening out there," he says.
>
> One strange thing that is happening out there is the appearance of the so-called "superbaby movement". . . mothers and fathers are flashing vocabulary cards at their toddlers . . . and feeding them a diet of mathematics and Johann Sebastian Bach to boot. Glenn Doman, . . . is considered the reigning prophet of the superbaby movement. He has proclaimed that "our individual genetic potential is that of Leonardo, Shakespeare, Mozart, Michelangelo. . . ."
>
> In the United States, the top 2 percent of some 46,112,000 children are classified as gifted.

The number of "gifted" children among the 314 Institutes' early learners upon entering school is

109 or, 34.7 percent. The chances of that happening by accident are as remote as finding a tie tac hidden in the sands of the beach at Atlantic City.

We must remember, however, that the "gifted" children who turned up in our survey are average kids selected by their parents before their fourth year of age to participate in The Institutes' early learning program; some children, before they were born.

5

Real Kids, Not Just Percentages

Sarah has developed such a strongly positive and mature out-look on life that she became a role model for the entire class. She loved her teacher, her classmates, was and is an outstanding student, and was loved by them in return.

As well as excelling in every aspect of schoolwork, she has the self-confidence to be herself. Consequently, others follow her lead, and every class she has been in tends to be high achieving as a group.

Judith Harris
South Hempstead, N.Y.

Not all of the kids in our survey turned out to be gifted, of course, but, as we noticed in the last chapter, an unexpectedly large number of them did turn out that way, as compared to the number of gifted children in the general population. Some of this general population had been stimulated when they were young, some had received a modest amount of input, and others had been allowed to get whatever their environment accidentally and incidentally provided. Still other children, regretfully, had been entirely neglected during their preschool years. This understimulated general population was what our surveyed early-learners were compared with.

Not neglected, thankfully, was little Kimberly Watt, of Colorado, one of our surveyed kids. When she entered this world with many birth problems, her mother was cautioned that the little girl might never attend regular school classes. Starting while Kimberly was a tiny baby, her mother, Lee Watt, after attending the Better Baby course, engaged in the early-learning program with her daughter.

Kimberly, now fourteen, has a real love of learning. School reports cite how well she pays attention and concentrates. When she was seven, the school's achievement tests and and those of the Denver district put her at post-high-school in several areas, with her lowest achievement score being 4 years advanced of her age. Kimberly's IQ on the WISC-2 is in the top 2 percent.

Another Institutes' early-learner, Matthew Israel, entered school in Costa Mesa, California, at five. His parents, Alan and Rebecca, had him evaluated because of certain concerns they had about school behavior. Psychologists agreed that "Matthew is a gifted child who is not being treated like a gifted child."

They recommended an advanced program, one which would be able to keep him engrossed, the kind that would keep leading him to ever-more sophisticated levels of knowledge, well beyond the usual classroom fare. In other words, the maturity of his specific curriculum should match his higher-level curiosity and intelligence.

Earlier, when he was four-years and two-months old, Matthew's mental age was measured at six years and two months. He had achieved an Intelligence Quotient of "145 + 13" on the Stanford-Binet Intelligence Scale, Form L-M. According to the examiner, that score placed him in the "Very Superior range of intellectual functioning, and it indicated that Matthew exceeded 98.9 percent of the children in the standardization group for his age."

The examiner asserted that the measure was a valid measure of intellectual abilities. In addition, Matthew demonstrated strengths in a variety of areas. He was "verbally adept, defined words accurately and combined them successfully into sentences." His facility with language was greater than most pre-kindergartners, and he "comprehended verbal relationships in a meaningful way." Matthew demonstrated no major areas of weakness. His overall performance significantly exceeded that of "most children in the normative sample used for comparison and was indicative of well-developed cognitive skills which will enhance academic functioning."

In Anaheim, California, nine-year-old Brett Butler was tested for gifted programs. School officials decided he "daydreams too much to go into the gifted classes, although he is at the top of his percentiles." The psychologist declared that Brett "lacks the anxiety about learning he'd need to compete with the other gifted kids." Despite that astonishing observation, the school placed Brett in classes above his entry level for reading since they could not deny that he was indeed advanced.

Isn't it wonderful that Brett thinks learning is fun instead of being anxious?

In Normal, Illinois, the school psychologist placed six-year-old Jeni Christianson's IQ at 150. The official asserted that Jeni must "guess well," because it was not possible that someone her age could perform so brilliantly. So much for school psychologists who believe that if the child has a high I.Q. that their own test must be wrong!

More astute officials in Grand Prairie, Texas, were quite correct in assessing little Michael Lester's intelligence. They stopped after the nine-year-old boy had reached the 210 IQ level. Michael was tired and "further testing would serve no purpose." The psychologist stated Michael was "unusually gifted—gifted in all areas—well-rounded plus socially comfortable and mannerly."

In Simi Valley, California, the score of yet another Institutes' child in our survey, Tucker Ross, at seven years of age, was better than 99 percent of the national norm group. The Unified School District issued the report that Tucker "had achieved better than 99 percent in Total Language, better than 99 percent in Total Mathematics, better than 99 percent in Science, and better than 99 percent in Social Studies." Tucker has continued to excel in all areas, in all subjects. He is the only one in the whole class—gifted 4-5 combination—who scored all 99s.

In the Southeast, in Coral Springs, Florida, Elizabeth Aleman is now in a gifted class. The teacher bubbled while describing the eight-year-old child in a conference with the Board of Education: "I wish you could meet her—she's just a delight to be with!"

On the East Coast, in Rosemont, Pennsylvania, Michael DiBattista had attended the Evan Thomas Institute International School through the fifth grade. At the time our questionnaire was dispatched, Michael was going to public school when he was referred for psychological evaluation. The purpose of the assessment was, "to determine whether he would benefit from participation in the Challenge Program for intellectually-gifted students." The psychologist stated,

> *Michael is a ten-year-old sixth-grade student who is presently enrolled in Algebra with eighth-grade students. All of his teachers report high level of work and consistent achievement in their classes. He is described as "bright, energetic, enthusiastic, and intellectually curious." He presently plays the violin and participates in swimming, among other avocational activities. He is a young man of accelerated mathematical skills.*
>
> *In seventh grade, as a participant in the 1991 Mathematics and Verbal Talent Search that included the ablest seventh-grade students in the*

*Talent Search Region, Michael scored "higher
than the average college-bound twelfth-grade student on the College Board's Scholastic Aptitude
Test."*

In conclusion, the professional report empha-
sized that Michael "had been exposed to a number
of accelerated contents in mathematics and the
sciences."

In the nearby suburb of Lansdale, Pennsylvania,
in seventh grade at only eleven years of age, Eve
Sandler, who had participated in The Institutes'
early-development program with her mom, Karen,
scored in the 97th percentile on the ERB Comprehensive Aptitude Achievement Test. Consequently, she was invited to take the SAT's early and
become a member of the coveted Johns Hopkins
University Talent Search '91.

Gifted eight-year-old Clinton Radenbaugh, of
Glendale, California, rises very early and reads the
newspaper. He's obsessed with baseball, loves statistics and the math of it. He recently observed, "Moms
make us intelligent and Dads make us brave."

When he entered his current school at age 11,
Cosimo Sherman, of Los Angeles, California,
tested at the twelfth-grade level. (Usually, a student
is seventeen or eighteen by grade twelve.) Cosimo's
advanced score didn't mean too much to him; he
thought it was funny. His teacher commented:
"He's incredible. He's phenomenal, really. He's an
outstanding student, very creative, with a sense of

delight in everything he does. He's well-liked and has a great sense of humor, kind of an ideal kid. He's just a brilliant person."

Still another Institutes' early-learner in the survey, Jack Giesecke Johnson, in Leander, Texas, placed in the upper 1 percent in almost every major or broad category in the California and Iowa Achievement Tests. At the end of fourth grade, he scored in the early eighth-grade level in math, at twelfth grade in reading, and twelfth grade in language and just as high in other subjects.

At three-and-a-half years of age, Jenny Raim, of New York City, was tested for entry into Hunter Elementary, a school for the gifted. She tested on the nine-year-old level in many parts of the Stanford Binet IQ Test. The tester believed little Jenny would have scored higher in some areas but the test only goes up to nine. Socially, she is loved by her teachers and her peers, and she shows great empathy and caring for others around her.

When entering school at five-years of age, Christopher Borecky, of Merrick, New York, scored a 153 IQ. Understanding of situations and use of logic in solving problems had always been considered advanced by professionals, and "he has a photographic memory."

In Palm Beach, Florida, Chase Polan's mother, Susan, has begun to engage in the early-learning program all over again with younger son, Benjamin. Many indications reveal that big sister Chase, eight years old, was affected by The Institutes' program. The best result has to do with confidence and independence. "She was tested on the genius level, and her school and sports' life have been superb." But her mom comments, "She's just a kid who does a lot of things very well."

Laura Sugarwala, of Lancaster, Pennsylvania, was ahead of her class when she entered school at age six. She loves learning, is very respectful and cooperative, and has played violin in the school orchestra since second grade. "Laura has a lot of friends but, in many ways, is more mature than her peers."

At six years of age in first grade, surveyed Institutes' early learner Pacien Mazzagatti, of Blue Bell, Pennsylvania, was tested for the gifted program which he enjoys very much. Scoring 100 percent word recognition and 100 percent comprehension, he was placed at the sixth-grade level in reading. The school officials did not test him beyond that level in reading and the fourth-grade level in math.

Pace enjoys the gifted program and meeting new people. In 1988, his eleventh year, Pace scored in the 99th percentile in reading and the 98th percentile in math on the Metropolitan Achievement Test. He's described as "a delightful boy with energy and curiosity in abundance." Now at fourteen, he works with a mentally handicapped student. Pace exhibits maturity and understanding, and is a very creative problem solver. Obviously, the purpose of this enlightened opportunity to help a disabled child is to heighten self-awareness and sensitivity towards others.

Alycia Hillman, of Laconia, New Hampshire, having begun her Institutes' program while a tiny baby, is now in school and designated "gifted." At eight months, she spoke in sentences. Ten months later, she was already reading signs; for example, "Potatoes 39 cents per lb." After another six months of early opportunities to learn, "at two years of age, she began writing love notes."

In Springfield Township School District, Erdenheim, Pennsylvania, two brothers who had participated in The Institutes' off-campus program, Aaron Greenfield, eleven years old, in fifth grade, and David, seven, in third grade, were placed in the "Enrichment Class."

Aaron was cited for his problem-solving and critical thinking abilities, and received kudos for his contribution to the Continental Math League. He was named "Springfield's Second Highest Scorer," having scored 99s for reading comprehension, vocabulary, concepts of number, math computation, math applications, and social science on the Stanford 7 Plus. His complete Battery Total was 98.

Aaron's mother, Marilyn, had asked younger brother, David, how he felt about learning to read before he entered school. David replied, "I'm glad because I can read books sooner."

In their "Annual Review," the School District announced that David had qualified for the Enrichment Program based upon classroom performance and the results of an individually administered intellectual evaluation. On the Binet Intelligence Scale he scored 148. School officials remarked, "David is a very bright and capable student. He participates in all of the activities, but he prefers doing science experiments or computer programs."

Two Institutes' early-learning brothers from Kettering, Maryland, Brian Rash, 14, and Michael, 13, currently attend Prince George's County Community College and play their violins in the County's Philharmonic Orchestra. Michael plays Mozart's Violin Concerto #4 and Brian plays Mozart's Violin Concerto #5. As the youngest members of the Washington, D.C. youth orchestra, they toured China and Taiwan in 1986. Both are members of the Casals String Quartet. Mom reports that introduction to music early has "been extremely valuable to the successes they enjoy now as young violinists."

The brothers are healthy and love to swim. Having participated in the early-development program with mom and dad when they were two and three, Michael and Brian are now the youngest students in their college. Astronomy professor Chris Hunt, says, "They have a natural curiosity. They maintain a high interest, a genuine interest in many different subjects. They're not just going through the motions."

Their mother, Billie, observes, "I think we're the average family who took a special interest in our kids. We enjoyed learning together, and this has created a special bond between my husband and me and the boys which is priceless."

Also in Maryland, two more Institutes' early-learn-

ing brothers, 10 and 12, (Mom requested their anonymity) received the following letter from the Department of Psychology of Johns Hopkins University:

Congratulations on your magnificent performance on the SAT in January! Your scores are
remarkable in the following respects:

1. Extremely few persons score 700-800M
   (Mathematics) or 630-800V (Verbal) before age 13. Only 5 percent of college-
   bound male 12-graders do as well as
   700M, and only 5 percent of them do as
   well as 630V. Less than 1 percent of them
   have a V + M total of 1440, and barely 1
   percent have 1390.
2. Few families have two children attaining the
   700M or the 630 V criteria. None but yours,
   so far as we know, has two attaining both.
3. — is only the second person below 11
   years of age to attain both. The other
   youth, a 10-year-old in North Carolina,
   tied him on V (650) and scored 10 points
   more than his 740M.

You have great learning potential for virtually anything you wish to master.

That kind of learning potential was also demonstrated by young Anthony Johnson whose parents,
Pamela and Robert, had attended the very first

Institutes' How To Multiply Your Baby's Intelligence course, and had gone home to carry out a most exciting early-development program with their new baby.

When Anthony was fourteen, in May, 1991, he passed the three-day entrance exam to Winchester College, England. This is a test devised and used only by this school. The subjects are: French, Greek, Latin, chemistry, physics, geography, history, science, English, mathematics and scripture. The test is considered to be twice as difficult as the Common Entrance Exam used by Eton College and Harrow School.

On the same day, back in the United States, the University of Denver Talent Search Program notified Anthony's parents that their son had received the award as highest achiever.

Another Institutes' early-learner, Matthew Richards of Lakeland, Florida, entered the pre-medical program at Lakeland Regional Medical Center when he was fifteen.

Eight-year-old Alyssa Ann Wolf attends a school for gifted children in Hopkinton, Massachusetts. She reads at least a book a day. Her ability to problem-solve has been called "phenomenal."

With grades A+ across the board, ten-year-old Ron Roeder, of Hulmeville, Pennsylvania, is registered in Neshaminy School District's Mentally Gifted program. Among his school peers, he placed first among Young Inventors USA. He is interested in conservation of natural resources, the United States National

Park System and backpacking. He qualified for state championship with a 50.8 all-around score and is a member of the United States Gymnastics Federation. Confident, assured and responsible, Ron joined the public school system as someone would join a country club. He exclaimed, "It's fun and a great place to meet people!"

Ron's younger brother, Zachary, seven, also an avid Institutes' early-learner, is likewise registered with the mentally gifted program. He's considered the most popular boy in school. Currently working toward his black belt in Karate, he swims, runs, and is "concerned about spaceship Earth."

In Puerto Rico, James Michael Betancourt has earned a 4.0 average, all A's, since entering kindergarten at five. In second grade, he was reading at the ninth-grade level. In fifth grade, in the opinion of his teachers, "he is *sobresaliente*, a genius." They assign him to help children who need remedial help. James "has an entire wall in his bedroom covered with awards and certificates."

In Miami, Florida, six-year-old Aimée González was evaluated by the School Board and placed in the Gifted Program for exceptional students. Quickly, she was skipped to second grade. Her sister, Yvette, having engaged in The Institutes' early-development program when she was younger than Aimée, was evaluated before her sixth birthday and recommended for instant second grade placement. Mother reports, "She just loves it, and is always ready to help others in need."

In Seattle, Washington, another Institutes' early-learner, Teddy Smith, at six years of age when he entered first grade, scored at the 99th percentile in the Total Complete Battery (all subjects) of the Metropolitan Achievement Test. His scores had been compared with those of other pupils of the same age across the nation. Teddy's teacher placed him at the seventh-grade level in reading.

Teddy was one of the youngest in M-2, the School for Gifted Children. "He was happy and secure."

In October, 1987, having just passed his seventh birthday, Teddy Smith composed the following lines:

The Shell

The beautiful shell,
the swirly shell—
on its roads I walk.
On the road of swirly shells
in the pitch dark night.

His mother, Paula , reported, "Teddy is usually the first in his science class to find a workable solution to a problem. Even in a class of gifted children he shines."

6

As Parents Tell It

*If men and women are to understand each other,
to enter into each other's nature with mutual
sympathy, and to become capable of genuine com-
radeship, the foundation must be laid in youth.*

Havelock Ellis
The Task of Social Hygiene

What happened to the home-taught early
learners socially when they got to school? In
many ways, this was the bottom-line question.

In our society, the matter of getting along with
other people is of agonizing importance. For
many parents looking to the future, this social
aspect of the child's life is of primary concern.
Years ago, when parents attending our courses
asked the question about how their kid would get
along with other children, we all thought it was
an American anxiety. Then, when course participants from France, England, Malaysia, Colombia,

Sweden, and Italy—from all the continents in the world—posed the same question, we became convinced that nationality had nothing to do with it. All parents all over the globe shared the same worries: Would their kids be considered "eggheads?" Would the other kids be intimidated by their superior abilities?

The children described in response to the survey were, for the most part, popular children who shone not only in academics or physical areas, but in all three tightly interrelated domains: social relationships, sports, and schoolwork.

The children were neither "nerds" nor "jocks," nor "snobs." But, in the same way that each of us parents is proficient in our own special way, so many children had developed exceptional talent in one or more of the three spheres: intellectual, physical, or social.

SOCIAL SKILLS

Following are extracts from parent comments concerning abilities developed by their children in dealing with teachers, friends and acquaintances.

The parents often chose the word "sensitive" when describing their children:

". . . his sensitivity to those around him and other such areas which are so difficult to measure have been the serendipities of being involved . . ."

"... *is very kind and sensitive to the needs of others.*..."

"... *shows great empathy and caring for others around her....*"

"... *continues to be a very sensitive, warm and loving child who still wants to be read to and cuddled, and cries over injured animals....*"

"... *is also a very sensitive child at school. He is the elder statesman; caring for many of the younger children....*"

"... *He is a beautiful, caring, sensitive intelligent person....*"

"*He is sensitive, charming, understanding and kind.*"

"... *socially very caring and considerate.*"

"*Ron's attitude toward people is extremely sensitive, understanding beyond his age the needs of the poor and destitute.*"

"... *it is the essence of Michael as a human being that amazes me most, and makes me proud to be his mother.*"

"... *a sensitive and caring person who has all the tools to help make a difference—a positive difference—to our world.*"

How well had their children accomplished the ticklish problem faced by all of us: getting along with other people? Parents tell us:

"The best result has to do with her confidence and independence."

"People enjoy being with my children."

"She seems to be less inhibited than the kids her age."

"The major benefit has been the profound and lasting shape given to Teddy's personality. . . . Teddy is certain he will be able to do anything. . . . He is relaxed and confident anywhere he goes. . . . He is willing to try anything, and does not give up if he does not succeed right away."

"She enjoys school and has a varied range of ages in her peer group, . . . is well-liked, confident and sociable."

"She is bright and very social, and actually getting into the psychology of dealing with people. . . . She is truly loved by her teachers and her peers."

". . . her friends cover the whole spectrum."

"She entered [school] very smoothly, was excited about, and loved the interaction with the other kids."

INTELLECTUAL SKILLS

Achievements in reading, language, math and other school subjects are of clear importance once a child enters school. The following parents and teachers touch upon these academic concerns:

"All of the mothers and teachers are now asking me what I have done with James to put him so far ahead. He writes long stories while the others are struggling with words . . . We are one of the rare families who taught our child to read at 6 months. He was a super reader at age 2."

"He is the smartest child I have taught in 30 years. He remembers everything he hears and reads. I am amazed."

One day last year at a school Assembly, the principal asked the student body (K-8) what "catastrophe" meant. When, after a minute, no one's hand went up, a little first-grader stood up and said, "When something big happens that you don't want to happen happens."

The whole assembly began to applaud. The child was Zack. The whole school knows Zack and he gets a lot of attention because of his abilities and his sweet unpretentious personality.

"Your daughter is absolutely wonderful, was it something you did, or was she born that way?"

"She is an extremely bright, curious child who absorbs information like a sponge; her ability to memorize from hearing information once or twice amazes witnesses."

"He talks to adults in a very intelligent fashion and, as a result, gets more than his fair share of attention from them."

"[Jenna] loves learning, loves people, interacting with them, receiving new stimulation. She enjoys herself and others."

"I know that young children have a great curiosity and desire to learn, but it is more than that. As a nursery school teacher, I see a difference between Adam's interest and the interest expressed by the kids in my class. It just goes beyond that."

"There is not a day that goes by when one of them doesn't do something bright and ingenious. I have had a great deal of contact with hundreds of other kids who haven't had the advantage of [The Institutes'] early-development program, and there is definitely a difference. The kids who've had the advantage of an early learning program seem more alert and questioning than their peers. It's almost as though you lit a fuse in them."

PHYSICAL SKILLS

Here are brief observations from parents concerning how their children performed in gym, in schoolyard sports, in various school and community athletic events—in brief, attainments by their children in the physical realm:

Jonathan Altschuler *"has fantastic eye-hand coordination."*

Kara Atienza is *"a talented gymnast and is presently a member of the Philippine National Women's Team. She trains 5 hours a day under a top-rated elite coach from the United States."*

As an eight-year-old, Jeni Christianson *"finished ahead of the entire Bloomington High School girl's cross-country team in a 500-meter race."*

Jonathan Emrich, six years of age, is *"a very bright, happy, physically-fit little boy. His sister, two and a half years younger, is burning up the track. She wants to do everything he does."*

Pacien Mazzagatti *"passed the deep water test his first year at camp, well before entering school. He was three years old. Pace was enrolled in gymnastics class for three years. At six, he started Karate. He now has a blue belt."*

Sheldon Quan-Wong is *"in very good physical condition, exhibits excellent coordination and speed."*

At seven, Teddy Smith runs seven miles nonstop

regularly with his friend. He could dive beautifully at age six. He was an advanced beginner in skiing before entering school.

Sisters Alayna and Megan Thompson are excellent swimmers and divers, having started well before school entry. Also, in their preschool years, they roller-skated, jogged two and a half miles, engaged in gymnastics, ballet, tap dance, and bike riding. The summer when she was four years old, Alayna took Red Cross lifesaving. She passed the course due to her excellent water skills, but she could not be certified because they believe the "age of reason" is six.

For Kehar Thornton-Gill, *"sports seem to be the center of his life. He participates in soccer, basketball, taekwondo, tennis, swimming, etc., etc."*

Mrs. John A. Henry of Sierra Vista, Arizona, was acutely aware of her daughter, Jennifer's, timidity. The little girl was especially shy and insecure outside the home when she was very tiny. Mrs. Henry exposed her to outside activities like gymnastics, dance, swimming, and even part-time preschool—to get her comfortable with other children and teachers.

Nowadays, *"Gymnastics is her forte and she feels very secure performing a balance beam routine in front of 150 people."*

MUSICAL SKILLS

With the abandon of a litter of kittens frolicking with a ball of yarn, The Institutes' early learners had surrendered themselves to the sheer joy of playing their musical instruments. Utter enjoyment grew into dedication, then evolved into ability and skill and, for many, intense love and deep satisfaction. As with the numbers of children classified as "gifted" and the numbers of children evaluated as "excellent," numbers far beyond proportions in the general population, so an outsized group of the children in our survey laid claim to the title "musician." They thereby added enchanting melodies, harmonies and rhythms to the richness of their lives and to the lives they touched.

Mothers and fathers provided us with examples of the talent developed by their children:

"Both children play the piano and I am learning piano."

"JoAnna, nine, has such a special musical ability. Her violin playing is superior. People are in awe of her playing, even her school. She won four music awards last year, and the only Golden Award in the entire school district."

". . . plays organ beautifully. We have kept the music program going and are thrilled to have two fine violinists and two fine pianists."

"Colleen, thirteen, auditions for the Philadelphia Orchestra competition in March of this year and we're real proud of this."

"She's outstanding in the arts and music. . . . Very creative and exceptional."

"They all started violin at the age of two. They love to perform. I would say they demand participation in everything. Last October they joined the Greater Miami Youth Symphony."

"Anthony, ten, continues to study violin, plays in the school orchestra, sings in the school choir."

"Sean, who shows a tremendous love for the violin, is involved in numerous competitions. His violin teacher spends a great deal of time with him in addition to his regular lessons."

"She is a wonderful human being—as well as bright, physically excellent, and musically superb."

"In his spare time he plays soccer, tennis, and enjoys playing music on his keyboard."

"Jason now plays the piano and trumpet, as well as the violin. His brother, Micah, now plays the electric bass and the alto saxophone, as well as the violin."

"Kimberly doesn't remember not having a violin as

she started that at eighteen months. She loves classical music, opera, ballet."

"Jonathan, twelve, has sung with the Texas Boys' Choir, learned piano, etc. His younger brother, Steven, ten, has written music lyrics since three years and at nine, wrote musical notes in an organized manner."

"She's played violin in the school orchestra since second grade."

"The other kids come over and want to know how to play our flute, piano, and violins."

At the Wissahicken Middle School in Pennsylvania, Pacien Mazzagatti, at thirteen years of age, accompanies the Suzuki Strings, performs with the Competition Jazz Band, and plays clarinet in the concert band. He's been a semi-finalist at the Stravinsky Awards International Piano Competition in Illinois.

Pacien was awarded a merit scholarship to Westminster Conservatory in New Jersey, he was chosen to perform at the Honors Recital of the New Jersey's Music Teachers Association, and was selected for the second time to be concerto soloist at Andrews Music Festival, Andrews University, Michigan.

ARTISTIC SKILLS

The Institutes' early-development program had

also introduced the children to the plastic arts, to drawing and painting and sculpture. In a world of beauty and color and imagination, the kids continue to glow. Parents were delighted to share with us the artistic talents of their children:

"She is a very talented artist and we have hired a professional art teacher to give her lessons in painting and sketching. She has already done many beautiful paintings."

"Marin wrote, produced and directed her own play at age 6. Much of Marin's work is art, drama, creative writing and reciting poetry."

As man lives not by bread alone, so our early-learners live not restricted solely to achievements in the world of academe, nor to prodigious feats in the realm of sport, nor to successes in the social arena.

They have also graced the years of their lives with enriching plastic arts, with bright poetry, resplendent drama and heavenly wordless dimensions of sublime music.

WELL ROUNDEDNESS

"Well-rounded" is a term applicable to most of the early-learners in our Institutes' survey. Skimming parental reports reveals that most of the kids have in common a great sense of humor. They can tell, as well as appreciate, a good joke; they can give and take good-humored teasing. They've also read lots of books, and can do math. Beyond academic and physical achievements, they're gentle, modest, affable. They're considerate of the feelings of others; they don't put on airs, and are congenial and friendly. They can either laugh and play, or be sad; it all depends on how appropriate the action is. They're all these things: physically excellent, intelligent, wise, and kind. In other words, they're well-rounded.

In each of the areas, physical, intellectual, and social, the same names keep cropping up: they're the same kids, doing all those things.

Early learners who excel in reading, math, and other school subjects are the identical youngsters who execute cartwheels, aerials, and vault over balance beams with the grace of Olympic stars. Multilingual boys and girls who play the violin and act in Shakespearean plays, are the same kids who knife through the swimming pool like young porpoises.

In general, however, while most do well in all realms, each child shines especially bright in his own favorite area. Having our favorite areas is what makes us unique as human beings. Were it otherwise, everyone liking and doing exactly the same things, every domain precisely balanced with every other domain, life would surely be as boring as a mashed-potato sandwich.

For example, in art, the characteristic of being slightly off-balance is what differentiates a great portrait from an ordinary painting. So it is with gourmet cooking. There, salt, pepper, spices, herbs, in just the right proportions, distinguish fine cuisine from humdrum fare. Too much sugar makes a dessert too sweet, too cloying.

If a child is "too good," and flaunts his excellence, eyebrows shoot up; you're put off. If he gets all "A"s, but spends all out-of-school time with textbooks, you tend to consider him a grind. If he's too serious all the time, can't relax and have some fun with the other kids, you tend to consider him a nerd. But if he does his thing superlatively, whatever it happens to be, does it beautifully and effortlessly; if he regards his performance as something all people could do, and if he can take time out for play, that's what being "well-rounded" really means.

Being a well-rounded kid also means that, occasionally, he has the right to be just plain silly, to just "let go," as long as the silliness doesn't get out of hand, leading to somebody getting hurt and ending up bawling. In short, he has the right to enjoy the exhilaration of being young.

That kind of gaiety was much in evidence back in 1981 when our team escorted boys and girls of the Early Development Program to Bogotá, Colombia to present the How To Multiply Your Baby's Intelligence course. Of course, their mothers came along to help us.

On the first day of the course, the bell sounded a ten-minute break period at the end of one of the fifty-minute sessions. The mothers and their little early-learners had just participated in sessions demonstrating to the Colombian parents how to help very young children learn to read and do math.

Out the kids scooted, to an enormous sun-drenched veranda in front of the auditorium. There, eight thousand feet above the jungle, the thin air was crystalline; a mild breeze, scented with perfume of tropical flowers wafted over concrete squares painted red and gold. Under watchful eyes of one of their moms, the kids raced around playing tag. Joyful shouts, mingled with uncontrolled giggling, resounded under the equatorial sky. These were the same children who had been politely demonstrating their intelligence just moments before. When the bell rang again, ending the break, the children continued to play. Colombian parents returned to their seats in the auditorium, and Glenn Doman resumed lecturing.

Just like those kids back then, when our surveyed home-taught early learners had reached school, their flexibility and resilience to be all business one minute, and relax and have fun the next, helped them meet the challenges of school and life. These kids were also well-rounded.

Here are a few examples of typical, well-rounded kids:

Colin Carnahan *"excelled in the private school, graduated from there at the end of eighth grade, and entered a much more traditional college prep private school for 9th grade. He excels there also, usually making the honor roll, playing in all four sports offered (football, basketball, track, and baseball) as well as being involved in just about every other activity in the school. He has a quick delightful sense of humor and strong sense of justice."*

Covell Day, of Sewell, New Jersey, in a program for the talented and gifted, is a straight "A" student. She has earned a place in an accelerated math and reading class and has won the library reading contest three summers in a row, completing over 500 books in the three contests. Covell enjoys ballet and tap, baton, gymnastics, jazz, tennis, and Spanish.

Mrs. Suzanne Bischof of Mountain Center, California, reports of her early-learning boys: *"They have a heightened sense of duty."* She also said, *"They're responsible and knowledgeable in caring for the animals and maintaining our homestead."*

Pamela Wright of Fredonia, Wisconsin, confides, *"My kids, with their knowledge of art, nature, etc. have information that others didn't even know existed, which surprised all of us."*

Yet, while our Institutes' home-taught early learners do have so many characteristics in common, they are very different from each other, as different as the flowers, shrubs, and trees in any well-stocked arboretum. Still, the following characterizations, culled from the parents' copious, open-ended comments, do create a lovely mosaic of the children who:

are *"interesting and imaginative"*;

"communicate well";

"love language deeply";

command *"an advanced vocabulary and vast knowledge base"*;

"never lack ideas";

"can talk with anyone about any subject";

are *"incredibly creative, inventive, and come up with keen observations"*;

"build the toys";

"reason well beyond their age level";

are *"disciplined"*;

"cooperate";

"set positive goals";

"concentrate on their work";

are *"persistent and complete their projects"*;

are *"inquisitive"*;

"exhibit a rage to learn";

are *"motivated by a tremendous thirst for knowledge"*;

"express a strong interest in the arts";

manifest *"a broad view of the world"*;

demonstrate *"a happy, excellent, positive attitude"*;

are *"friendly, charming"*;

reveal *"a delightful sense of humor"*;

are *"sound"* emotionally;

are *"considerate," "mannerly," "anxious to please"*;

"enjoy other children's successes";

"have patience with the slow pace of other children, and are not critical of others";

are *"not worried about other's opinions"*;

are not *"show-offs," "don't brag,"* and *"are not big-headed nor pompous"*;

are *"well adjusted mentally and spiritually"*;

are *"leaders who excel without seeming effort"*;

exhibit *"an excellent attention span"* and *"can sit*

still in an academic environment and attend to a learning situation for extended periods.";

display memory skills frequently called *"amazing, and photographic";*

"easily adapt and are resilient";

use *"advanced logic"* and *"think analytically";*

"have a phenomenal ability to problem-solve, and demonstrate 'different' thinking patterns."

"feel that social aspects are important and enjoy the social aspect of school";

"believe relationships are important";

"fit in with the mainstream of life, easily, yet with a great deal to offer, quietly";

"discount the good and bad in dealing with everyday people";

"are quickly accepted by and respected by peers and older children";

are *"independent"* and *"willing to try anything";*

are *"responsible for their own learning";*

are *"discriminating in the kind of students to associate with";*

"choose to adopt social skills of adults, rather than those of nine-year-olds."

As reported by the surveyed parents, teachers also weighed in with their enthusiastic comments about The Institutes' home-taught early learners:

Cosimo Sherman's teacher observed, *"He expresses a sense of delight in everything he does."*

Kristen Stoermer's teacher called her little student, *"a super-thinker."*

Eric Fisher's teacher declared, *"He doesn't need to be reminded over and over about things, and I haven't heard him say, 'I can't do that.'"*

Scott Campbell's teacher exclaimed, *"He's a winner in all areas: academically, physically and socially."*

Not all of the children, of course, possess all of the above traits, but most of the characteristics, however, do accurately describe the vast majority of the surveyed Institutes' early-learners.

OPEN-ENDED COMMENTS

The questionnaire had requested specific information to most effectively answer the query raised by parents who had attended the How To Multiply Your Baby's Intelligence course: "What's going to happen when my kid gets to school?"

Yet, it was also important that the surveyed

parents not be restricted to answering terse questions alone; instead, it was clear that they ought to be granted the opportunity to describe, in their own words, how they felt about having participated in the early-development program advocated by The Institutes. We, therefore, requested that they provide us in as much detail as they wished, their thoughts about the way their child had been affected and their reactions. Responses were comprehensive and enthusiastic. Typical comments follow:

From Sheri Bandy, of Sequim, Washington:
I was thrilled to have been part of your program and to share that with my daughter. It has been one of the most rewarding aspects of motherhood. My son is now enjoying the benefits of our teaching at home and is thoroughly enjoying it.

As far as I can see, there are no negative aspects to your program, especially because it is designed and can be altered by the parents, as they feel necessary.

From Doris S. Betancourt, of San Sebastián, Puerto Rico:
I not only love my child, but I like my child. I love being around him because he has opened my eyes to so many things in my environment that I either took for granted or didn't even realize existed. He asks questions that astound people. His thinking pattern is so different than mine. He is a unique individual.

From Claudia Borecky, of Merrick, New York:

It was highly beneficial. My son cruised at 6 months, walked at 9 months, read the newspapers at 2 years old, and has consistently progressed in math. His I.Q. was tested at 153. His understanding of situations and his logic has always been advanced and he has a photographic memory . . . It is easier for a baby to learn to read. Because of his early learning, he will never have trouble with school.

From Jeanne Clark, of Battle Creek, Michigan:

. . . doing the early learning program with my kids was and continues to be very rewarding. It gave us the opportunity to create a bond between each of us that may never have been there. It taught me to be aware of what my child was hearing, seeing, being told by others, etc.

I have had many parents say to me, "Don't you think you're pushing your kids too much?" My response is often, "You don't have to push a child to learn. Just give them the opportunity!"

From Leslie Daane, of Reno, Nevada:

Brad has a great love for learning which his early development program helped instill. His favorite birthday gift was a globe. His teacher even commented on his creativity and imagination. For one show-and-tell he took in a picture of a time machine he drew and described it for them. . . . She did comment that he was the brightest in her class. . . . I know what I have done has made a difference.

From Rev. Sarah L. Darter, of Winter Park, Florida:

Nikki's early learning program:

—fostered a love of learning on her part; my respect for her early intelligence.

—made me aware of my authority/right/privilege/duty to teach and stimulate my own child.

—taught and modeled specific methods to use.

From Eugene duPont, of Hockessin, Delaware:

I love working with my girls and it's the most important thing I have done. They have strong foundations and can now grasp life and do what they wish with it.

From A. Benton and Lixlia Edmons, of Reisterstown, Maryland:

I.B. enjoys many activities, which most children have not had opportunities to learn about, due to his reading and understanding of a wide variety of subjects.

He can explain many complicated things on almost a technical level. The guide at Hoover Dam, four years ago, was amazed at I.B.'s knowledge of architecture of dams, and of the production of electricity.

From Linda M. Gray, of Locust Valley, New York:

Baron is a very interesting, humorous, considerate child, well-liked by his peers and elders. He can easily converse with anyone about any subject and I am sure it was due to all the bits of information learned at an early age. He was one of the first to read in his class and absorbs books with excellent comprehension.

From Janet Gauger, of Glenside, Pennsylvania:
One thing is certain–they are both varied, interesting and physically-fit kids who share our enthusiasm for many subjects.

I doubt that they would have the musical expertise or foreign language abilities without the program, as these were areas lacking in my early education.

Above all, the program gave me the legitimate means to be a "professional" mother, an unpopular career ten years ago. Now, I see more women making the choice of home vs. careers, and without condemnation.

From Lisa Hardegree, of San Diego, California:
My son is doing very well in all the subjects, especially reading, math and science. He is very much interested in every subject that I present to him.

I am very happy and pleased that I did the program with my son. If I ever have another child, I have no doubt that I'd do the same all over again. There is nothing more rewarding than teaching your child.

From Peggy Hilgers, of Clearwater, Florida:
I feel that through the How To Multiply Your Baby's Intelligence Course I was not only able to have a great early program with Erik, but I also had the knowledge and criteria to be able to select a school which would be optimum for him to ensure his happiness and success in school and life.

He loves learning and school and at age 7 is developing into quite a likeable, responsible, ethical and able person.

From Karen Hoffmeister, of Fallston, Maryland:

I believe Ryan only benefited from his early learning program. It gave us a lot of good, happy, sharing moments together. I have got to believe it gave him the knowledge and the confidence in himself that he has today.

From Rita Falk Johnson, of Plantation, Florida:

Tara's attitude toward life and enthusiasm towards learning I feel was very much enhanced by her early learning program. It has carried over to David her younger brother more from Tara than us. David brachiates and attempts many physical exercises with enthusiasm and strong determination due to Tara's positive approach nurtured by the program.

From Richard Joy, of Fairbanks, Alaska:

The benefit to Nathan, and his younger sister, of the early learning program is probably impossible to calculate. Both Nathan and, even more so, his sister, are very bright kids who love to learn.

. . . I have a very good feel for how my kids' brains work. This may not sound like much on the surface, but I think the best thing the early learning activities ever did for me, and my kids, was to give me a fabulous insight into how kids live and learn. This has enabled me to view the world through their eyes, and to understand their behavior.

Far from pushing kids, this approach uses love and parental involvement to not hold them back.

From Catherine Mansfeild, of Salt Lake City, Utah:
I remember fondly the times Christian and I spent learning together. He was always eager to learn and enjoyed as much as I the many, many visual "Bits" of information.

From Lonnie Menter, of Nampa, Idaho:
When she was eight years old, from July to September, 1976, Janel read 600 books in a 10-week period and won Nampa's Summer Reading Contest.

Mrs. Barbara Montgomery, of Rosemont, Pennsylvania, mother of Michael DiBattista, one of the children in our study, filed lengthy and informative accounts of what they had been doing together. Just before this book went to press, Glenn Doman received a letter from her and here shares it with us:

Mike is now almost thirteen—just two more months—but chronology is so deceiving. He has come through this year in the public school in all honors classes in the eighth grade, and as a member of the Challenge Program. He has made the honor roll every report period. He is looking forward to next year in high school where he has chosen his own curriculum in the honors program, but then also decided to take part in the Scholar's Program, the highest academic challenge in the school. The student has to request participation, and then get the recommendations by his current teachers. Mike got them all.

This past year he was also the quarterback of the football team, at times running his own plays, and simultaneously the first violin in the orchestra. I have enclosed a newspaper article about a large area orchestra of which Mike was an invited member; the comment I have highlighted is interesting for it deals with the belief that kids must be limited in their choices.

The day of one of the rehearsals Mike played fifteen pieces from Corelli to Mozart to Bizet, hopped in the car and went to his swimming meet, where he won every event to be undefeated for the season. Two days later, the performance was held— the kids had to take directions from thirteen different conductors! Quite a challenge, and a beautiful concert.

Sometimes it's difficult to find out just what Mike has accomplished, for he is not one to talk of his own achievements. One day he did tell me about the 100 on his Algebra II test, but then I had to find out in the monthly school mailing that he had the highest grade in his school for the Pennsylvania Mathematics League contest and was participating in the state-wide competition.

Another student's mother from another school let me know that Mike was one of the highest scorers in the area French competition held at Chestnut Hill Academy. And his, "Oh, Mom, I forgot to tell you . . . " about being selected by his peers to be part of the team to compete in the national Knowledge Master Open.

But that will have to wait, for Mike is going to the State championships for swimming this weekend, and next week will be competing in the Eastern Zone All-Star Meet, the highest United States swimming achievement for someone of his age.

Then, this summer he will be going to the South to work for a week building homes for Habitat for Humanity with his church youth group. . .

Three years after Susan Polan had replied to the original questionnaire and told us about her daughter, Chase, she wrote again from Florida:

The program is extraordinary. Not only has Chase's school and sports life been superb, we share a greater capacity as people through our learning experiences. Our son, Benjamin, is now enjoying the pleasures and pursuits of the early learning program.

From Elaine Poole, of Sylmar, California:

Tom is an incredibly creative, inquisitive kid. His ability to "figure out" how things work, or why something is the way it is easily exceeds that of the average child his age. His vocabulary is also advanced. The Bits helped quite a bit on this, and his physical prowess was further improved as the program continued.

Creatively and physically he excels. He is a very

determined and confident child. I'm sure the program helped Tom immensely on acquiring the skills he now has. We did do lots of physical exercise and bit cards.

From Terri Rice, of Perkiomenville, Pennsylvania:
What fun teaching Melinda has been! I am always amazed to meet parents (and professionals) who think teaching your own kids could somehow be harmful. To whom, I wonder? My only regret is that the years went by much too quickly.

She is a wonderful human being, as well as bright, physically excellent, and musically superb. What better gift could I possibly have dreamed of giving the world!?!

From Mark Sherman, of Philadelphia, Pennsylvania:
One of the greatest benefits of the early learning program is that when either of the boys is presented with new material of any sort in any subject area, he is able to assimilate, understand, and apply it without further explanation.

From Patsy Sogioka, of Redlands, California
I feel Michael was helped and I wouldn't want to have missed out on what I learned from you for anything. The most benefit is for my daughter, however. I was just barely pregnant with her when I went to The Institutes. She will start school next fall, possibly in the second grade. Her reading skills are good, her math skills are excellent. She has the understanding and grasps math

concepts much faster than my son, who was 3 when I took the course. I started her on math at 8 weeks. She doesn't remember not having a violin, as she started that at 18 months. She loves classical music, opera, ballet, ice skating, gymnastics.

I have often wished I could fill my house with mothers and their babies and help them see all the potential that is there.

From Colleen Wang, of Alta Loma, California:
With my second son, Nathaniel, we started at day 1. Very early, he was way ahead. He always checked out over double his age at the pediatrician's. He crawled at 4 mos., walked at 10 mos. He always had a clear idea of what it was he wanted to do. He could read before he could walk, and loves math.

I find it most interesting and relevant that his specific areas of excellence were the areas we both enjoyed in the program. He excels without seeming effort.

The program saved my sanity because it had taught me how to find and structure answers to his demands. At all times we treated him as an equal and knew he always understood us.

From Lynn Williams, of Plano, Texas:
There is no doubt that my child has definitely benefited from the IAHP program:

1) The program has given him a real joy for learning any subject and enthusiasm for any subject.

2) Being able to read well has helped him enjoy school and appreciate all that the teacher presents to him.

There are no early struggles or negative feelings about school and learning.

3) The program has given him a great deal of self-confidence.

4) The program has given him an excellent capacity for memorizing and understanding facts.

5) Early reading has given him a concentration ability not seen in other children.

6) The program has helped develop a close mother-teacher relationship with my children.

7

"What Will Happen to the Kids in Life?"

I have but one lamp by which my feet are guided, and that is the lamp of experience. I know of no way of judging the future but by the past.

Patrick Henry
March 23, 1775

When he was Education Editor of *The New York Times*, Fred Hechinger reported results of a sixteen-year study involving deprived children in Illinois. Hechinger wrote that a small group of African-American children had been provided with a modest stimulation program at age three. The kids grew up with markedly greater success than a comparable group that didn't have early help.

When the children in that study had reached nineteen years of age, the differences between the two groups, the ones who had just a bit of stimulation while they were very young and the ones who didn't, were stunning in all areas, academic, social, and domestic. Hechinger concluded, "The economic benefits to themselves and to society are incalculable."

And what about the 314 children who had followed an Institutes' early-development program before they entered school? How will they do in life? Most of them are still in school. What will happen when they leave, some to go to college, others to create lives for themselves away from academe? All studies on the subject suggest that success in school often does predict success out in the big wide world, success in all realms.

As our survey was winding down, four instances of this kind of happy future outcome for Institutes' early-learners came to our attention. The first is a mother, once an Institutes' early-learner, now at home full-time helping her baby to learn to read and many other wonderful things. The second is a busy internist. The third is an international executive who flies around the world for a large corporation. And the fourth is an award-winning journalist who is also the mother of infant twins.

The full-time mother is Jennifer, daughter of an old colleague of mine, Bill McLeod. Bill had accomplished a highly important statistical task for The Institutes at least fifteen years ago just as our formal early-learning program was picking up steam. Then, he moved on.

Jennifer was a tiny girl at that time. She had

learned to read when she was two-and-a-half. One day shortly before this book was being put to bed, Bill popped into the office and, during the course of reminiscences, he brought us up-to-date concerning Jennifer.

In school, "she never worried about grades," although she did complete a four-year college in three years, graduating cum laude. "She did it without any summer school by 'klepping' several courses studied on her own."

Bill exulted, "She's turned into one of the most well-adjusted people I know. She's not interested in being a career woman; instead, she has one child, and is pregnant with the second. She is following the early-learning ideas that helped her. The importance of raising her own kids is uppermost in her mind."

Leaving, Bill stopped, turned and added, "Oh, I have to tell you an incident I vividly remember. It happened when she was three-and-a-half. That summer, she had read 235 books in quick time. I wasn't positive she had really understood all of them until one day, there she was, sitting in a corner looking at a piece of paper and chuckling."

"Curious, I looked over her shoulder and saw she was reading a list of all the books. Obviously, she was appreciating the memory of the stories. I still wasn't fully convinced, so I pointed to some titles at random. She remembered every one of those stories."

He ended, "The one thing that stands out is that today she's really a well-rounded individual capable of doing anything well, and she gives a lot of service to the community."

Also giving service to the community are medical doctors. We learned about Dr. Keith March when, a number of years ago, Eleanor V. March wrote a letter to Glenn Doman. She wrote:

I have read with considerable interest both your letter on the subject of teaching one's baby to read and the information put out by the Encyclopaedia Britannica on your Better Baby Reading Program. This brought many pleasant memories back to both my husband and myself, and I brought out your book, How To Teach Your Baby To Read and noted the date was October 26, 1964.

At that time, Mrs. March's son, Keith, was sixteen months old. With great enthusiasm, she and her husband set out to teach Keith to read. They printed their own cards initially, quite of few of them, and launched the program when Keith was seventeen months old. In her words, "The results were absolutely mind boggling."

Keith graduated from St. Francis College as Valedictorian of his class in Chemistry and Biology at age fifteen. He attended Indiana University as a double medical major and science student (combined MD/PhD) and received his Ph.D. degree at age twenty; two years later, he was awarded his M.D., at age twenty-two, probably the youngest man in history to have earned the double doctorate .

Mrs. March wrote,

To say that we have enjoyed Keith's accomplishments immensely would be a gross understatement. There is no doubt that his ability to read early has done much to enhance his progress throughout the years and, incidentally, socially he is a well-adjusted person—has never had any serious problem in dealing with his peers, who have always been between five and seven years older. He has always been accepted well by his classmates, teachers, and professional associates.

Keith was, and still is, an accomplished organist. He built a full-size theater organ at age nine, and he is also an accomplished guitarist and singer. During undergraduate years at Indiana University, he sang with his own folk group at St. Paul's Catholic Church in Bloomington.

Twenty-seven years after his mother had helped him learn to read using Glenn Doman's book as a guide, in the early nineties, Keith himself wrote to us. He is now a practicing physician and married. His words:

My mother was a dedicated homemaker who helped me learn to read at seventeen months of age. By the age of three to four, I was able to read newspapers and magazines, and at four, read Grimm's classic collection of fairy tales. Reading has been one of my favorite pastimes since those early years, just as the sciences have attracted my greatest interest ever since

*curiosity was aroused by my father, a patent lawyer
and chemical engineer. He presented simplified ex-
planations of the new wonders that surrounded me.
My earliest interest in medicine was sparked by a
child's 'doctor's bag kit,' and reading about biology
and medicine led to a consistent desire to practice
medicine.*

In school, Keith was advanced one year between
the second and third grades. At St. Richard's he
received the highest math award in sixth grade, the
highest science and English awards, as well as
Outstanding Student award in the seventh grade,
his last pre-university level.

He skipped all high school, won first place at the
Mississippi Regional Science Fair in 1974 with a
project entitled, "Wankel vs. V-8 Engine," and first
place in the Mississippi State Science Fair in 1975.
There, he dubbed his entirely new project, "Magic
of Photography."

Keith successfully passed the ACT college entrance examination in 1975, after which he was
accepted by Mississippi College and St. Francis
College in Fort Wayne where he enrolled. His
G.P.A. of 4.0 kept him consistently on the Dean's
List. In 1977, he received the biology award for
top academic achievement as a sophomore. He
was awarded the Dr. Wilkie B. Rice Academic
Scholarship for premedical students the next
year, and again earned the highest honor Dean's
List Award.

In 1978, he was accepted by four medical schools, and offered a scholarship and stipend for a combined degree program by each of the first three. He graduated in May, 1979, with a B.S. double major in Biology and Chemistry.

He entered Indiana University, took the first two years of medical school courses and completed the requirements for the Ph.D. in biochemistry. He received his M.D. with Highest Distinction, May 12, 1985, and selected internal medicine as his career specialty, because "it focuses on direct patient contact and permits a broad approach to medicine from a general physiological/biochemical perspective of both diagnosis and treatment."

Keith's hobbies include golf, tennis, swimming, and photography—enlargement and development of his own color prints. He has a long-standing interest in astronomy. He's enjoyed instructions in flying small airplanes, and has earned his private pilot license. On October 1, 1988, he was married to Sarah Perin, who plays the French horn and is a "very supportive wife."

Both Keith March and Jennifer McLeod had learned to read using Glenn Doman's approach while they were very young. The following story tells of two other of his early readers now grown up and out in the real world.

Earlier, I spoke of producing, back in 1966, the television series *Wordland Workshop* to help three-year-old children learn to read. This series integrated Glenn Doman's recommendations for helping mothers teach their babies how to read. This program was used in a carefully-controlled study to test the effectiveness of such an effort.

The mother of one of the children in the "experimental group" of that study, Nina Robinson, has brought us up-to-date about her son and his younger sister:

> *When Damian was three years of age, and Lauren was one, we lived in Hackettstown, New Jersey, where we were able to get reception for the Philadelphia television stations. You had a program, Wordland Workshop, with Wendy the Wallaby, and you taught children to read. Damian was registered in your program, Lauren was too young to be registered but learned anyway.*

Damian and Lauren always headed their classes throughout most of their school careers. They both entered Science High School at the age of twelve in Newark, New Jersey, where the Robinsons were living at that time. Like Keith March, Damian was named Valedictorian of his graduating class. As a National Achievement Scholar, majoring in chemistry, he entered Harvard at sixteen years of age.

He was twenty-two when he received his M.A. from Johns Hopkins University School of Advanced International Studies, after which he worked as Congressman Peter Rodino's legislative correspondent, and spent one year in Bologna, Italy. Our most recent update on the siblings tells us:

Damian, at 30, is a director at American Express Bank (International). He has travelled to England, Spain, France, Germany, Switzerland, Italy, the Soviet Union, Indonesia, China, Japan, Canada, Mexico and South America. He reads, writes and speaks Italian, Spanish, Portuguese, German, French, Russian, Indonesian, a little Urdu, and Chinese. He wants to be able to eventually speak all of the major languages in the world.

When his sister, Lauren, was in her junior year of high school, she received a scholarship to Milton Academy in Massachusetts. She had already been earmarked as Valedictorian of the Science High Class of '81. Also graduating at sixteen, she entered Princeton. She earned her M.S. degree from Columbia University Graduate School of Journalism when she was twenty-one years of age. Now, at twenty-eight, she is mother of baby twins who are having fun with our early-learning program. As journalist for the Dallas Times-Herald, covering the government beat, she received many awards for her reporting, and has been recorded in the Congressional Record twice. She now writes for the Boston Globe.

Mrs. Robinson adds:

Damian and Lauren were always very normal kids. They did all of the things other kids do. Their teachers always expected to find them in a corner, by themselves, reading, when they saw their academic record, but they were always involved with the other children, and were always very popular in school. They are both very nice young people and are very concerned about humanity. They try very hard to make a valuable contribution to mankind. Damian is still very interested in the sciences, especially environmental issues. Lauren is very concerned about social issues. They're great kids!

In Mrs. Robinson's eyes, they're still "kids," despite the fact that Damian is obviously a man of the world, and Lauren is unquestionably a mature woman, now a mother herself, having earlier accumulated a wealth of worldly experience developing human interest stories and digging out the truth in the labyrinth of government.

But, more than that, and more important, not only in Mom's eyes, but surely in the eyes of the people with whom they've come in contact, they're "great" kids. It's clear that Damian and Lauren possess the essential qualities that, in a genuine sense, illustrate what this book is all about.

8

Conclusion

The Institutes for the Achievement of Human Potential, a group of nonprofit, federally tax-exempt institutes in the highest category, are committed to the significant increase of the ability of all children (brain injured and unhurt) to function in the physical, intellectual, educational and social realms.

For nearly a half century, The Institutes have devoted time to researching the problems of child development. . . . We have been able to ascertain and to validate the significant developmental sequence. . . . In well human beings the process of brain maturation, which begins at conception and which is clearly evident at birth, is virtually complete by eight years of age.

The speed at which this process takes place varies widely from human being to human being. It can be demonstrated easily that this process of neurological maturation can be slowed slightly by certain cultural factors which prevent good brain organization. This process can be slowed considerably by certain environmental deprivations which create neurological dysorganization. This process can be halted completely by brain injury. In a neurological sense all children can be embraced in a continuum which ranges from the severely brain-injured child without neurological organization at one end of the spectrum to the superior child with extremely good neurological organization at the other end of the spectrum.

The work of the individual institutes has established clearly, and contrary to popular belief, that children who are far below average in this continuum can be raised to average levels. Indeed, the work has proved conclusively that even severely brain-injured children may be raised to average levels by the employment of non-surgical approaches to the human brain itself.

When significant numbers of brain-injured children had been raised to average and, occasionally, far above average brain levels, it became apparent that the process of neurological maturation can be be speeded as well as delayed and that this speeding can be accomplished by certain simple non-surgical procedures.

The use of these procedures on normal children has enabled us to augment developmental progress significantly in infancy and childhood. As a result, we have demonstrated that neurological maturation, which was formerly considered a static and irrevocable fact is instead a dynamic and ever-changing process.

From: IAHP Statement of Objectives, 1962

When our team became aware of the overriding importance of the human brain, and of the preeminence of the early years, we created the discipline of Child-Brain Development from many different fields: functional neurology, anthropology, pediatrics, physiotherapy, physical education, sociology, early education, history, and physicians representing a dozen specialties.

Now, in this last decade of the twentieth century, we are all Child-Brain Developmentalists, fellows and members in good standing of the International Academy for Child-Brain Development. We devote our days to learning how the human brain grows, and how the human brain develops. We are practical, results-oriented clinicians for hurt children and their parents; and results-oriented teachers of well children and their parents. During the past fifty years, we have compiled hundreds of people-years of experience working with both groups.

Our labors have yielded precious fruit. We have learned elegant lessons about the brain, and precious lessons about what we can do to help it function better. For brain-injured children these lessons have been virtual life-savers. (See *What To Do About Your Brain-Injured Child* by Glenn Doman) For tiny well children these lessons have meant an enhanced opportunity to become excellent in intellectual, physical and social realms. (See *How To Multiply Your Baby's Intelligence* by Glenn Doman)

From among these many lessons, we have gleaned the following six facts that, for parents of tiny well children, are the most vital and most valuable:

1. The brain of a new human being grows explosively, but less quickly each succeeding day, from conception to six years of age.
2. The brain grows by use.
3. The brain runs everything.
4. The potential of our human brain is unimaginably great.
5. We can increase the possibility of attaining ever-higher levels of that potential by starting early in the life of a young child, while the brain is growing at a fantastic rate.
6. This early start is most effective when initiated and carried out by the tiny child's mother and father. And only when applied with joy and love.

Having learned these lessons well, our team has resolved to teach parents to be sensitive to their tiny children, especially, to be aware of the six essential stages of brain growth and development:

1. Visual brain growth and development.
2. Auditory brain growth and development.
3. Tactual brain growth and development.
4. Mobility brain growth and development.
5. Language brain growth and development.

6.   Manual brain growth and development.

We have resolved to teach mothers and fathers how to help their children benefit from their heritage as human beings by providing them with an understanding of how the brain grows and develops, and the tools to use to help their babies profit from their innate, sponge-like ability to learn everything.

For the parents of the 314 children in our survey, competence was the name of the game. The mothers and fathers set out to make their children competent. They trusted that competence would bring about confidence. And they felt that, in turn, confidence would give their kids security. Others would feel comfortable around them. Their children wouldn't have to adopt bizarre behaviors to gain attention, or to "prove themselves."

They wanted their children to be independent, truly the goal of all loving parents. And, in a way, independence on the part of the kids would give the parents a new opportunity to do their own thing, to afford them time to continue enriching their own lives.

During those fleeting first years, parents expressed incomparable love for their children in ways surpassing the ordinary. They shouted and carried on with glee; they kissed and hugged, made sure their kids always had nutritious meals and warm shelter, introduced their sons and daughters to reading, math, music, swimming, running, gymnastics, music, the arts, human empathy, and to as much of the world's immense treasurehouse of knowledge as they humanly could. They knew that, deep down, their kids sensed an unspoken message of love that all the attention, time, and richness of The Institutes' early-development program were sending.

How much of this program is it advisable to do? Here's what Glenn Doman advises on the last day of the How To Multiply Your Baby's Intelligence course:

> Do exactly as much as you are comfortable doing. If you enjoy teaching your baby how to read for three minutes a day, then teach him to read for three minutes a day. Don't let anybody talk you into doing more. He'll be a world better off for it.
>
> If you are comfortable teaching your daughter five minutes of reading and five minutes of encyclopedic knowledge a day, then do it and don't let anybody talk you into a jot more.
>
> If you can and do wish to be a full-time professional mother or father, then the sky's the limit.
>
> And don't let anybody talk you into less.
>
> If you cannot do it joyously, then don't let anybody alive talk you into doing it.
>
> If you can't wait to get started, then don't let anybody alive talk you out of doing it.

Our report has ended.

We are able to conclude, based upon parent comments, that the 314 children in our survey are kids whose eyes shine. They are children endlessly interested and interesting. They're imaginative. They're kids you like to talk to; they listen (all adults like kids who listen) but, more than that, they stick with the give and take of conversation. Their questions are fresh although, sometimes, biting. They're rapt, attentive to solid answers, tickled when they learn something new. Often, they can't contain themselves and giggle uncontrollably. You enjoy being with them.

They continue to manage emotions well; they deal smoothly with all age groups and, perhaps most importantly, they persist in being kind and caring and sensitive, far more than others the same age.

They're well-rounded. They are socially popular, handle school subjects, play most any sport. They know a lot of things in many different areas; are at ease in the schoolroom, on the playground, at home, at a neighbor's house, anywhere.

They're kids for all seasons.

They're "Renaissance Children."

At the beginning, in their first year in school, they were well ahead of other kids the same age. Still ahead, they're now proceeding through the grades in many different kinds of schools in many different places.

Their parents, who know them better than anyone else in the whole world; their teachers, who spend at least five hours each day with them during the week; their friends, on whose opinions the kids themselves place great value; all agree:

Kids who start ahead, stay ahead.

Afterword

What a piece of work is man, how noble in reason,
how infinite in faculties; in form and moving, how
express and admirable, in action, how like an
angel, in apprehension, how like a god: the beauty
of the world! The paragon of animals!

William Shakespeare

Scholars, scientists, and saints throughout history insist that we human beings have been operating at only a fraction of our powers; they have urged us to go for it, to reach for the stars. Yet, until now, in our era of atomic magic and space travel, we have ignored the plea as little more than a preposterous dream. But the winds of change are blowing hard. In the light of breakthrough insights and solid experience, this dream of a higher quality human being has a genuine chance of becoming real.

In one way or another, we've all thrilled to the

dream of changing man. Have you ever watched a bright-eyed child of four gazing in wonderment as a soap bubble floats lazily in the air? The gay iridescence of its surface pleases him, and he muses about its fragility, perhaps even wishes that such a beauty might not vanish as quickly as he knows it must.

Later, as a mature adult, he may regard the same bubble philosophically. He may compare it, with a wee bit of imagination, to that dream he once held of helping fellow human beings improve their condition. He may remember, with a sting of remorse, the trauma when the bubble burst, and the weight of man's inadequacy, in the face of seemingly insuperable obstacles, settling heavily on his shoulders. He may remember philosopher Ortega y Gasset's observation that, "every life is, more or less, a ruin among whose debris we have to discover what the person ought to have been."

The ruin does not have to happen. Preventing it from happening is hope, a bracing perfume. Hope dissipates nauseating fumes emanating from the television nightly news; hope, the glorious loom on which we weave generous dreams.

Referring to the stuff of which dreams are made, Anatole France asserts:

> Out of dreams come beneficial realities. Utopia is the principle of all progress, and the essay into a better future. We cannot ignore our Utopias. They exist in the same way that

north and south exist; if we are not familiar
with their classical statements we at least know
them as they spring to life each day in our own
minds. We can never reach the points of the
compass; and so no doubt we shall never live
in Utopia; but without the magnetic needle we
should not be able to travel intelligently at all.
It is absurd to dispose of Utopia by saying that
it exists only on paper. The answer to that is:
precisely the same thing may be said of the
architect's plan for a house, and houses are
none the worse for it.

Utopia? A problem-free world? There is no such
place. The very meaning of Utopia is "Nowhere." St.
Thomas More had combined the ancient Greek
words "U" meaning "no" and "topia" meaning
"place," when he named his ideal society. A little
more than a hundred years ago, Samuel Butler wrote
Erewhon, which, with slight revision, is "nowhere"
spelled backwards. One of the most famous science
fiction writers of all time, H.G. Wells, wrote *Men Like
Gods* and another half-dozen tales of human societies
that cured all the ills of mankind. Much earlier, Plato
painted a perfect social arrangement; his *Republic*
was ruled by "philosopher kings." And only a half-
century ago, Bellamy's *Looking Backward* titillated
the imagination of college students.

Throughout history, legions of early social scientists envisioned and actually established utopias,
ideal societies. Their noble experiments—lofty in

intent, flawless in design—perfect communities for imperfect human beings. Names roll down from top to bottom, as if on a giant motion picture screen: the New England Puritan colonies, the Shakers, Oneida, Brooke Farm, Fourrier societies, the communes of the sixties, and on and on and on.

Each of them failed.

Most disappeared after the death of the original charismatic leader, the dynamic and persuasive visionary who had sparked his dream to life. Of lesser stature, followers fell to bickering, and the lovely experiment came undone, unraveling at the seams.

Fictional utopias of the future usually depict a society ticking along with the precision of a fine Swiss watch—too perfectly. For instance, Aldous Huxley's *Brave New World,* or George Orwell's *1984.* The heroes of these tales became tired of the bland existence that boasted all of the spice of boiled grits. They craved life peppered with challenge, perhaps even peril.

Chances are that particular yearning hitches a ride with our genes, that it's an itch inherited from our dangerously living ancestors. How else explain the wild thrill of a monster roller coaster, the elemental elation of mountain-climbing, the ultimate exhilaration of sky diving? Couch potatoes soothe a nearly universal ache to place one's life on the line; they watch Sunday afternoon football and get their kicks vicariously; they identify with modern-day gladiators in full fray.

You find young people who live in places where every day is bright and warm and sunny complaining. Once in Baja, California, when I praised the unchanging splendid weather, a yuppy real estate salesman, in an unguarded moment, confided, "Yeah, another miserable day in Paradise."

We human beings are the discontented species: restless, ever-searching for something novel, for something better. Were it not so, we'd still be either in the trees or grubbing out a precarious existence on some remote African savannah. Lewis Mumford explains why, up to now, utopias never succeeded. He writes:

> It comes to this then: our plans for a new social order have been as dull as mud because, in the first place, they have been abstract and have not taken into account the immense diversity and complexity of man's environment; and in the second place, they have not created any vivid patterns that would move men to great things. They have not been informed by science and ennobled by the arts.

We do want a better world, but we've got to inform our dreams by science and ennoble them by the arts. Somehow up to now, all we've managed to do is replace one set of distressing problems with others much more grievous.

Our innate restlessness has led to the shattering of many seemingly impenetrable barriers to human progress: scarce food supply, hostile environments, widespread pestilence. We've produced abundant food; built efficient shelter, attained optimal health on a large scale. But achieving equitable distribution of these products of human genius remains as perplexing as ever it was in Caesar's time. With the predictability of the planetary cycle, night following day, have-nots have rebelled against haves. Insurrections, disease, famine, innumerable and vicious crimes follow inescapably. All of these misfortunes might just possibly be the result of the lack of sufficient intelligence.

What is intelligence? Most of us sense the meaning, but because of overheated debate since the IQ was invented by Binet, shortly after this century began, we are confused when we have to put our feelings into words. Often after someone has done something ingenious or said something clever, we observe, "My, wasn't that intelligent?" If the same someone continues to perform the same kind of superior behavior consistently, we would probably say, "Now, there's an intelligent person!"

Actions count. What we do is far more important than the score we get on an IQ test. And what we do and how well we do it is usually a product of what we know, how much we know and the number of past opportunities we've enjoyed to apply that knowledge and experience successfully, or unsuccessfully. The more choices or options we can call on, the greater the chance we'll act intelligently.

Apart from our few inborn human instincts, everything we learn comes to us through our eyes, ears, tactile nerve endings, taste buds, and our sense of smell. Obviously, these sensory pathways to the brain have to be in good working order if we're to acquire knowledge. It is also true that how we move, use language, or use our hands depends on how well we've seen, heard, and felt the world. A definition of intelligence that makes the most sense is one that relies on the quality of these incoming and outgoing pathways to and from the brain. The healthier those pathways are the more information we'll receive. As Glenn Doman emphasizes frequently during The Institutes' How To Multiply Your Baby's Intelligence course, that information, together with our range of experience, determines the number of options we'll be able to select at any given moment.

Men and women who have as many options as possible to make the most intelligent choices will be, by this definition, superbly intelligent. These new human beings will see, hear and feel things the way they truly are. They will solve problems baffling to lesser mortals. They will radiate compassion and profoundly understand the human condition. In other words, these ideal people will have gone a long way toward achieving their human potential.

Are these most intelligent human beings possible? Or, like those never-to-be-achieved utopias, are they to remain forever unattainable? Nearly a quarter century ago, Glenn Doman imagined how the Missing Link might have envisioned a future being. Glenn wrote, "Tomorrow's man to survive would have to be more fleet of foot, more strong, more skilled with the weapons he had, in short, more like he was."

Doman then reflected:

> At this moment in history we can produce more capable children and thus children with greater knowledge and more options to deal with tomorrow's problems, tomorrow's needs and tomorrow's magnificent opportunities. It has been the pomposity of each generation to assume to make the next generation in its own image and thus solve today's but never tomorrow's problems. Is not the mere creation of a more capable child with more knowledge and thus more options in itself the creation of a superior man?

That "superior man" was also on the mind of the eminent scientist/novelist C.S. Snow. Snow predicted, "Men in the future may try to improve the quality of their lives through an extension of their responsibilities, a deepening of the affections and the spirit in a fashion we can only dimly perceive."

About future man, in the middle of the last century, Samuel Butler raised an extravagant question:

> Why may not there arise some new phase of mind which shall be as different from all present known phases, as the mind of animals is

that of vegetables? It would be absurd to attempt to define such a mental state (or whatever it may be called) inasmuch as it must be something so foreign to man that his experience can give him no help toward conceiving its nature.

Later, H.G. Wells shared Butler's vision. In *Men Like Gods*, he wrote, "These Utopians were passing beyond man towards a nobler humanity. They were becoming different in kind." From our vantage point, we can say that they were approaching their human potential.

What that potential is we just don't know. All we can do is try mightily to achieve it. I like to believe that The Institutes' early-learning children we've described in this book may be in the vanguard of those wonderful human beings who will erect grand societies, not utopias; rather, *some* place. Their marvelous human communities may emerge in a time closer than we dare dream.

On that glorious day, challenges will be in the form not of death-defying stunts; instead, they will be challenges to create great works of art, of music, of poetry, challenges to engage profoundly in man's unending spiritual quest. Down through the long train of ages, of all of the billions of people who have ever lived, only a few score thousand have ever used so much of our nearly infinite brain power to change the world. A handful, really.

A handful of people—but enough to have pro-

duced the Ten Commandments, to have polished
the brilliance of modern medicine, and to have
fashioned the miracle of America. This precious
handful of superb human beings had, in one form
or another, adopted as their creed the call to
action immortalized by Goethe:

Lose this day loitering, 'twill be the
*   same tomorrow.*
And the next, more dilatory.
Then, indecision brings its own delays,
*   and days are lost*
Lamenting over days.
Are you in earnest?
Seize this very minute what you can do.
Or dream you can.
Begin it.
Courage has genius, power, magic in it.
Only engage, and the mind grows heated.
Begin it,
And the work will be completed.

APPENDIX A

Institutes'
Early Learners

BB = Parents attended the How To Multiply Your Baby's Intelligence Course ("Better Baby" Course)

OC = Parents subscribed to the Off Campus Program

M/F	#	NAME	STATE/ COUNTRY	BB/OC
M	001	ACERRA, John	NJ	OC
F	002	ALEMAN, Elizabeth	FL	OC
M	003	ALLEN, Luke	TX	OC
M	004	ALTSCHULER, Jonathan	CA	BB
F	005	AMBERGE, Essence	GA	OC
F	006	ANDERSEN, Lindsey	CA	OC
F	007	ANDERSON, April	VA	OC
F	008	ATIENZA, Kara	Philippines	BB
F	009	BAKER, Alison	NJ	BB
F	010	BANDY, Melanie	WA	OC
M	011	BARKHORN, Charles	CA	OC
F	012	BARTON, JoAnna Lynn	PA	BB
M	013	BARNES, Adam	PA	OC
M	014	BARNES, Christopher	PA	OC
F	015	BARNES, Lacy	PA	OC
F	016	BARNES, Victoria	PA	OC
M	017	BASTOS, Rogerio	Brazil	BB

M/F	#	NAME	STATE/ COUNTRY	BB/OC
M	018	BASTOS, Ronaldo	Brazil	BB
F	019	BECK, Sharon	CO	OC
F	020	BERRY, Shauna M.	IL	BB
M	021	BETANCOURT, James M., Jr.	Puerto Rico	OC
M	022	BEZAZIAN, Justin	CA	OC
M	023	BISCHOF, Joshua	CA	OC
M	024	BISCHOF, Matthew	CA	OC
M	025	BLAIR, Alex	VA	OC
F	026	BONVILLAIN, Danis Joy	LA	BB
M	027	BOONE, Christie	CA	BB
M	028	BOONE, Paul	CA	BB
M	029	BORECKY, Christopher	NY	BB
M	030	BRAZIER, Brian	CA	OC
F	031	BROWN, Colleen	PA	OC
F	032	BROWN, Ellie	DE	BB
M	033	BROWN, Frederick	PA	OC
M	034	BROWN, John	PA	OC
F	035	BROWN, Katie	PA	OC
F	036	BRUMBY, Virginia	GA	BB
M	037	BUTLER, Brett	CA	BB
F	038	CAMPBELL, Cate	CA	OC
M	039	CAMPBELL, Scott	CA	OC
M	040	CAPURRO, Jeremy	NV	OC
F	041	CAPUTO, Adriana	PA	OC
F	042	CAPUTO, Cara	PA	OC
M	043	CAREY, Joshua	TN	BB
M	044	CARMEL, Michael	CA	BB
M	045	CARNAHAN, Colin	TX	BB
F	046	CARNAHAN, Elizabeth Ann	TX	BB
M	047	CASTELLINO, Sasha	CA	BB
M	048	CASTILLE, Chad	LA	BB
F	049	CHAN, Elizabeth	HI	OC
F	050	CHANG, Sara	PA	OC
F	051	CHARLES, Megan	PA	OC
M	052	CHECCHIO, Joseph	PA	OC
F	053	CHRISTIANSEN, Jenimide	FL	OC
F	054	CLARK, Andra	MI	BB
F	055	CLARK, Jierra	MI	BB
F	056	COHEN, Lea	NY	BB
F	057	CONKLIN, Elizabeth Anne	CO	BB
F	058	CONKLIN, Jill Ann	CO	BB
M	059	CONNER, Stephen	France	BB
M	060	COOPER, Eric	CO	BB
F	061	COOPER, Tanya	CO	BB

M/F	#	NAME	STATE/ COUNTRY	BB/OC
M	062	CORONEOS, Christopher	MD	OC
M	063	COSTIN, Travis	NC	OC
F	064	COVENTRY, Chloe	CA	BB
M	065	COVENTRY, Christopher	CA	BB
M	066	COVENTRY, Nicholas	CA	BB
M	067	DAANE, Bradley	NV	BB
M	068	DADOURIAN, Thomas	NJ	BB
F	069	DARTER-MARTIN, Nicole	FL	BB
F	070	DAVIS, Natalie	CA	BB
M	071	DAVIS, Pete	CA	BB
F	072	DAY, Covell	NJ	BB
F	073	DELMONTE, Juliana	CA	BB
F	074	DEMOSTHENES, Alexis	CA	OC
M	075	DESMARAIS, Paul	Canada	OC
F	076	DeVEAU, Vanessa	FL	OC
M	077	DIBATTISTA, Michael	PA	OC
M	078	DILLEHAY, Jeremiah	CA	OC
M	079	DILLEHAY, Zachary	CA	OC
F	080	DILWORTH, Crystal	CA	OC
M	081	DIMANCESCO, Marc Mihai	NY	OC
F	082	DOLAN, Amber	NJ	BB
F	083	DUPONT, Ishnee	DE	BB
F	084	DUPONT, Bjornen	DE	BB
F	085	DUPONT, Trilby	DE	BB
M	086	EDMONS, I.B.	MD	OC
F	087	EISENBERG, Arlana	LA	OC
F	088	EISENBERG, Cherina	LA	OC
F	089	ELKRIEF, Samantha	NY	OC
M	090	EMRICH, Jonathan	CA	OC
F	091	EXUM, Kaitlen	MA	OC
M	092	FALCO, Ernie	FLA	OC
F	093	FARNSWORTH, Marisha	CA	OC
M	094	FIGUEROA, Jared	MA	OC
F	095	FIGUEROA Leigh-Ellen	MA	OC
M	096	FISHER, Eric	IL	BB
F	097	FLEMER, Emma	NC	OC
M	098	FORHAN, David	CO	BB
F	099	FORHAN, Katherine	CO	BB
F	100	FORHAN, Lindsay	CO	BB
F	101	FRANCIS, Nicola	Bermuda	BB
M	102	GAINSFORTH, Zachary	CA	OC
M	103	GALE, Philip	FL	OC
M	104	GALLARDO, Benjamin	CA	OC
F	105	GAUGER, Michelle	PA	BB

M/F	#	NAME	STATE/ COUNTRY	BB/OC
M	106	GAUGER, Neal	PA	BB
F	107	GONZALEZ, Aimée	FL	OC
F	108	GONZALEZ, Yvette	FL	OC
F	109	GONZALEZ, Michelle	FL	OC
M	110	GRAMS, Joshua	PA	BB
M	111	GRAY, Baron	NY	BB
F	112	GREEN, Jessica	DE	BB
M	113	GREENFIELD, Aaron	PA	OC
M	114	GREENFIELD, David	PA	OC
M	115	GRYNOL, James	Canada	BB
F	116	GUE, Elizabeth	WA	OC
F	117	HAMILTON, Sarah Mae	IL	BB
M	118	HARDEGREE, Sinuhe	CA	OC
F	119	HARRIS, Sarah	NY	BB
M	120	HAWKINS, Kevin	CA	OC
F	121	HENRY, Jennifer	AZ	BB
F	122	HENRY, Laura	AZ	BB
M	123	HESLIP, Peter	MA	BB
M	124	HILGERS, Erik	FL	OC
F	125	HILL, Teagan	South Africa	OC
F	126	HILLMAN, Alycia	NH	BB
M	127	HILLMAN, Anthony	NH	BB
F	128	HILLMAN, Suzanne	NH	BB
M	129	HOFFMEISTER, Ryan	MO	OC
M	130	HOLLISTER, Daniel (Kellogg)	PA	BB
M	131	HOLSEY, Ronald	MD	BB
M	132	HORTON, Christopher	AZ	BB
F	133	HOUGH, Laurie	MO	OC
F	134	HURTAK, Christine	PA	BB
M	135	HURTAK, Michael	PA	BB
M	136	ILLINGWORTH, Charles	IN	OC
M	137	INGLIN, Adam	WA	OC
F	138	INGLIN, Autumn	WA	OC
F	139	IRELAND, Marin	CA	BB
M	140	ISRAEL, Matthew	CA	BB
M	141	JECK, Dustin	NE	BB
M	142	JENSEN, Stephen	WA	BB
M	143	JOHNSON, Anthony	CO	BB
M	144	JOHNSON, Jack	TX	BB
F	145	JOHNSON, Jamin	MT	OC
F	146	JOHNSON, Tara Alyssa	FLA	BB
M	147	JOY, Nathan	AK	OC
F	148	KAIFESCH, Jennifer	CA	BB
F	149	KATZ, Brandi	PA	BB

M/F	#	NAME	STATE/ COUNTRY	BB/OC
M	150	KATZ, Sean	PA	BB
F	151	KENT, Ashley	CA	BB
M	152	KIBLER, Christopher	NY	OC
F	153	KLEIN, Dana	GA	BB
M	154	KOENIG, George	PA	OC
F	155	KOENIG, Maryellen	PA	OC
M	156	LAURIE, Peter	England	OC
M	157	LAW, Zachary	PA	OC
M	158	LEE, Henry	CA	OC
M	159	LEFKOE, Blake	CT	OC
F	160	LESTER, Elizabeth	TX	OC
M	161	LESTER, Michael	TX	OC
M	162	LEVINGER, David	CA	BB
F	163	LINDSAY, Brooke	WA	OC
M	164	LIM, Brian	CA	BB
F	165	LIPPINCOTT, Heather	NJ	BB
F	166	LIPPITT, Elizabeth	GA	OC
M	167	LOFTUS, Andrew	NY	BB
F	168	LONGON, Mary	NJ	BB
M	169	MANSFIELD, Christian	UT	BB
M	170	MARINARI, Peter	PA	BB
M	171	MARTIN, Benjamin	CA	BB
F	172	MARTIN, Elizabeth	PA	BB
F	173	MARTIN-MORENO, Beatriz	Mexico	OC
M	174	MARTIN-MORENO, Enrique	Mexico	OC
M	175	MASCI, Logan	NJ	BB
M	176	MAZZAGATTI, Pacien	PA	BB
F	177	MCCARTY, Heather	PA	OC
M	178	MCCARTY, Paul	PA	OC
F	179	MCCARTY, Shana	PA	OC
F	180	MCCREERY, Maggie	CO	BB
M	181	MCKINNEY, Harry	PA	OC
F	182	MENTER, Janel	ID	BB
M	183	MILLER, Jason	Nassau	BB
M	184	MOULTRIE, Carl	CA	OC
M	185	MOULTRIE, Child #2	CA	OC
M	186	MUELLER, Adam	MD	OC
F	187	MURPHY, Sarah	CA	BB
M	188	MURPHY, Scott	CA	BB
M	189	MUTH, Edmund	CA	BB
M	190	MYERS, Alison	PA	OC
M	191	MYERS, Chip	PA	OC
F	192	MYERS, Ginette	PA	BB
M	193	NAKAYACHI, Yuuki	PA	BB

M/F	#	NAME	STATE/ COUNTRY	BB/OC
M	194	NEFF, Aaron	NY	OC
F	195	NEILSON, Erin	CA	BB
F	196	NEMIRO, Aria	AZ	OC
M	197	NOLAND, Joel	CA	OC
F	198	O'CONNOR, Tiba	LA	BB
F	199	O'HARA, Georgia	NJ	OC
M	200	OCHSNER, Kipp	NE	OC
M	201	ODOM, Christopher	CA	BB
M	202	OSMANSON, Benjie	CA	OC
M	203	OSMANSON, Dusty	CA	OC
M	204	PACK, Stevie	CA	OC
F	205	PALLAS, Donna	PA	OC
F	206	PALLAS Stephanie	PA	OC
F	207	PALLAS Michelle	PA	OC
M	208	PALLAS, Paul	PA	OC
F	209	PALLAS, Alicia	PA	OC
F	210	PALLAS, Kathy	PA	OC
M	211	PARRY, Robert	MA	BB
M	212	PEREIRA, Jock	PA	OC
F	213	PEREIRA, Molly Ann	PA	OC
M	214	PEREIRA, Josh	PA	OC
M	215	PERRY, Blake	PA	BB
F	216	PETERSON, Jill Allyn	AZ	OC
M	217	PETROPOULOS, Thomas	MD	OC
M	218	PETRUCCI, Adam	NY	BB
F	219	POLAN, Chase	FLA	OC
M	220	POOLE, Tom	CA	OC
F	221	POTTER, Crystal	NY	BB
M	222	RADENBAUGH, Clinton	CA	OC
F	223	RAIM, Jenny	NY	BB
M	224	RASH, Brian	MD	OC
M	225	RASH, Michael	MD	OC
F	226	RICE, Melinda	PA	BB
M	227	RICHARDS, Matthew M.	FL	BB
F	228	RICHMOND, Heather	CA	OC
M	229	ROBERTS, David.	PA	BB
F	230	ROBERTS, Lura Lee	CO	OC
M	231	ROEDER, Ronald W., Jr.	PA	BB
M	232	ROEDER, Zachary	PA	BB
M	233	ROSS, Tucker	CA	OC
M	234	ROSSITTO, Ryan	PA	OC
F	235	ROTHERMEL, Jesse	CA	BB
F	236	ROTHERMEL, Lindsay	CA	BB
F	237	RUTTKAY, Jenna	OH	OC

M/F	#	NAME	STATE/ COUNTRY	BB/OC
F	238	SACKETT, Joan	WA	BB
F	239	SANDLER, Eve	PA	BB
F	240	SCHEPPMANN, Elizabeth	IA	OC
M	241	SCHWARTZ, Marcus	TX	OC
F	242	SCHWARZ, Jennifer	CA	OC
F	243	SEARS, Alissa	CA	BB
M	244	SEURET, Tyson (Retzloff)	CA	BB
M	245	SEXMITH, Jonathan	FL	BB
M	246	SHERMAN, Cosimo	CA	BB
M	247	SHERMAN, Jason	PA	BB
M	248	SHERMAN, Micah	PA	BB
F	249	SLANK, Erika	TX	OC
F	250	SMALL, Bright	PA	BB
F	251	SMALLEY, Denelle	CA	BB
M	252	SMITH, Teddy	WA	OC
M	253	SMITH, Colin	WA	OC
M	254	SOGIOKA, Michael	CA	BB
F	255	SOGIOKA, Kimberly	CA	BB
M	256	SOLARI, Brian	CA	OC
M	257	SOLARI, Vincent	CA	OC
M	258	SOMERSON, Jeremy	IL	BB
F	259	SONNICHSEN, Vanessa	CA	OC
F	260	SONNICHSEN, Autumn	CA	OC
M	261	SORRELLS, Riley	CA	OC
F	262	STOERMER, Kristen	CA	OC
F	263	STONEBACK, Sarah	PA	OC
F	264	STONER, Catherine	DE	BB
F	265	STRATTON, Shelley	OR	OC
M	266	STREETER, Jonathan	TX	OC
M	267	STREETER, Steven	TX	OC
F	268	STRUMPELL, Elizabeth	CA	BB
M	269	STUEBER, Ryan	OR	BB
F	270	SUGARWALA, Laura	PA	BB
M	271	SUGARWALA, Child #2	PA	BB
F	272	SULLIVAN, Tiffany	CA	OC
M	273	TAGERT, Adam	CA	BB
M	274	TARSITANO, Christopher	NJ	OC
F	275	THOMPSON, Alayna	CA	BB
F	276	THOMPSON, Megin	CA	BB
M	277	THORNTON-GILL, Kehar	AZ	BB
F	278	TONG, Elizabeth	Canada	OC
M	279	TONG, Eugene	Canada	OC
M	280	TSUKADA, Fumio	Japan	OC
F	281	VAN ARRAGON, # 1	Canada	BB

M/F	#	NAME	STATE/ COUNTRY	BB/OC
F	282	VAN ARRAGON, # 2	Canada	BB
F	283	VAN ARRAGON, # 3	Canada	BB
F	284	VAN ARRAGON, # 4	Canada	BB
M	285	VAN ARRAGON, # 5	Canada	BB
M	286	VAN ARRAGON, # 6	Canada	BB
M	287	VAN ARRAGON, # 7	Canada	BB
M	288	VAN ARRAGON, # 8	Canada	BB
M	289	VAN OVEREN, Joshua	MI	OC
F	290	VENNERA, Nicole	CA	OC
F	291	VOIGT, Kaiya	NJ	OC
M	292	WAGNER, Thomas	NJ	OC
M	293	WALDMAN, Alex	NJ	BB
M	294	WALDMAN, Zachary	NJ	BB
M	295	WALDRON, Chad	CA	OC
M	296	WANG, Jeremiah	CA	OC
M	297	WANG, Nathaniel	CA	OC
F	298	WATT, Kimberly	CO	BB
M	299	WEST, Bryan	MO	BB
F	300	WEST, Child #2	MO	BB
M	301	WILLIAMS, James W.	TX	OC
M	302	WILLIAMS, Ronald	CA	OC
M	303	WILLIS, Trevor	MD	BB
F	304	WILSON, Lisa	CA	BB
F	305	WOLF, Alyssa Ann	MA	BB
M	306	WONG, Sheldon	CA	BB
F	307	WOOLLEY, Sarah	NY	OC
M	308	WRIGHT, Matthew	WI	OC
M	309	WRIGHT, Child #2	WI	OC
F	310	WURZEL, Jill	NY	BB
M	311	X*, Child #1	APO, NY	OC
M	312	X*, Child #2	APO, NY	OC
M	313	ZELLAR, Duane	IL	OC
F	314	ZUPANCIS, Tracy	CO	OC

* Anonymity requested

BOYS: 170
GIRLS: 144
TOTAL: 314

APPENDIX B

Highlights of the How To Multiply Your Baby's Intelligence Course

Sunday

* Registration
* First Class Session
* Formal Tea

Monday

* The Objectives Of The Institutes
* Heredity And Environment
* Kids: The Myth versus The Reality
* Why Teach Your Baby To Read
* A Reading Demonstration By Mothers And
  Children Of The Evan Thomas Institute
* How To Teach Your Baby To Read

Tuesday

* How The Brain Grows
* What Is Intelligence?
* Potential Intelligence
* BITS Of Intelligence

Wednesday

* Mothers Are The Best Teachers
* It Is Good, Not Bad, To Be Highly Capable
* Teaching The Facts versus The Laws
* Kids And Instant Mathematics
* A Math Demonstration By Mothers And
  Children Of The Evan Thomas Institute
* How To Teach Your Baby Math

Thursday

* The Ontogeny Profile/Human Ontogeny
* The Visual Scale/Visual Development
* The Philosophy Of The Floor/The Mobility
  Scale
* A Gymnastic Demonstration By Mothers And
  Children Of The Evan Thomas Institute
* How To Make Your Baby Physically Excellent

Friday

* How To Teach Your Baby A Foreign Language
* How To Provide Your Baby With Good
  Nutrition

* The Institutes' Developmental Profile
* How To Teach Your Baby Music
* A Music Demonstration By Mothers And Children Of The Evan Thomas Institute
* Meet The Mothers
* A Philosophical Summary

Saturday

* The Off Campus Program
* "Always A New Beginning," a feature film about the Institutes (Nominated for an Academy Award for Best Full-Length Documentary Film)
* Certification and Graduation Ceremonies

All parents attending every session of the course will receive a certificate of qualification in Child-Brain Development at the Parent's Level. This certificate qualifies parents to use the knowledge gained during the week with their own children but it does not qualify parents or professionals to teach anyone else.

Eligible to take the course are all parents who wish to be superb parents and who believe that all babies and tiny children can perform at much higher levels than is presently the case. No academic degree is required.

APPENDIX C

Bibliography

Almy, Millie E. "Children's Experiences Prior to First Grade and Success in Beginning Reading." *Teachers College Contributions To Education*, No. 954, New York Bureau of Publications, Teachers College, Columbia University, 1949.

Aoki, Chiye, Siekevitz, Philip. Article, *Scientific American*, December, 1988.

Associated Press, "262 Billion Spent on Education," October 25, 1990.

Azimov, Isaac. *The Genetic Code*, New York: Signet, 1962

Barrientos, Tanya. "Figures on City's Public

Schools Tell a Tale of Failure," *Philadelphia Inquirer*, July 5, 1991.

Bennet, E.L., Marian C. Diamond, David Krech, Mark R. Rosenzweig. "Chemical and Anatomical Plasticity of Brain," *Science*, v. 146, pp. 610-619, October 30, 1964.

Bloom, Benjamin S. *Stability and Change in Human Characteristics*, New York: John Wiley, 1964.

Bower, B. "Academic Acceleration Gets Social Lift," *Science News*, Vol. 138, October 6, 1990.

Brim, Orville G., Jr., Jerome Kagan, (eds.) *Constancy and Change in Human Development*, Cambridge: Harvard University Press, 1980.

Bruner, Jerome S. *The Process of Education*, Cambridge: Harvard University Press, 1960.

——, et al. *Contemporary Approaches to Cognition*. Cambridge: Harvard University Press, 1957.

Brzeinski, Joseph F. "Beginning Reading in Denver," *The Reading Teacher*, vol. xviii, No. 1, October 1964, pp. 16-21.

Burr, H.S. *The Neural Basis of Human Behavior*, Charles Thomas, 1960.

Butler, Samuel. *Erewhon*, New York: AMS Press, Inc., 1968.

Calhoun, J.A. and R. C. Collins. "From One Decade to Another: a Positive View of Early Childhood Programs": *Educational Digest* 47, 44-6, Nov. 1981.

(In 1977, George Washington University compiled the results of more than 50 research and evaluation studies done since 1969.)

Campion, George C. and Sir Grafton Elliott Smith. *The Neural Basis of Thought*, New York: Harcourt, Brace and Co., 1934.

Carroll, Herbert A. *Genius In The Making*, New York: McGraw-Hill Book Co., Inc., 1940.

Castle, E.B. *Ancient Education and Today*, Baltimore: Pelican, 1961.

Chukovsky, Kornei. *From Two To Five*, Berkeley and Los Angeles, California. 1963.

Ciardi, John. "When Do They Know Too Much?" *Saturday Review of Literature*, May 11, 1963, p. 16.

Cousins, Norman. *Human Options*. New York: W. W. Norton , 1981.

Dart, Raymond A. M.D., *Adventures With The Missing Link*, Philadelphia: The Better Baby Press, 1986.

Degler, Carl N. *In Search of Human Nature*. New York: Oxford University Press, 1991.

Deutsch, C.P. and Deutsch, M. "Brief Reflections on the Theory of Early Childhood Enrichment Programs," *Early Education*. R.D. Hess and R.M. Bear, eds. Chicago: Aldine, 1968, pp. 83-90.

Dewey, John. *The Child and the Curriculum*, Chicago: The University of Chicago Press, 1902.

Diamond, Marian C. *Enriching Heredity - The Impact* of

the Environment on the Anatomy of the Brain, New York: The Free Press, Macmillan, 1988.

Doman, Glenn J., Janet Doman. *How to Teach Your Baby to Read,* New York: Random House, 1964; The Better Baby Press 1986; Avery Publishing Group, 1994.

——. "A Matter of Truth and Options," Human Potential, Vol 1, No. 1, 1967.

——, Janet Doman. *How to Teach Your Baby Math,* New York: Simon & Schuster, 1979; Avery Publishing Group, 1994.

——, et al. *Encyclopaedia of Intelligence,* Better Baby Press, IAHP, 1981.

——, Janet Doman. *How To Multiply Your Baby's Intelligence,* N. Y.: Doubleday, 1984; Avery Publishing Group, 1994.

——, Janet Doman, Susan Aisen. *How To Give Your Baby Encyclopedic Knowledge,* Philadelphia: Better Baby Press, 1980; Avery Publishing Group, 1994.

——, J. Michael Armentrout. *The Universal Multiplication of Intelligence,* Philadelphia: The Better Baby Press, 1980.

——, Douglas Doman, Bruce Hagy. *How To Teach Your Baby To Be Physically Superb,* Philadelphia: The Better Baby Press, 1988; Avery Publishing Group, 1994.

——. *What To Do About Your Brain-Injured Child,* New York: Doubleday, 1974; Avery Publishing Group, 1994.

Dryden, Gordon and Jeannette Vos, Ed.D. *The Learning Revolution*, Rolling Hills Estates, California: Jalmar Press, 1993.

Durkin, Dolores. *Children Who Read Early*, New York: Teachers College Press, 1966.

——."Children Who Learned To Read At Home," *Elementary School Journal*, 62, :15-18, October, 1961.

——. "Children Who Read Before Grade 1, A Second Study," *Elementary School Journal*, December, 1963.

Eiseley, Loren. *The Immense Journey*. New York: Random House, 1946.

——.*The Star Thrower*, New York: Times Books, 1978.

United Nations. *Encyclopaedia of World Problems and Human Potential*, Brussels, Belgium, 1989.

Fay, Temple. "Origin of Human Movement," *American Journal of Psychiatry*, 3:644-653, March, 1955.

Feinstein, Alvin. *Science*, October, 1990.

Fenner, Phyllis. "Reading, Like Charity, Begins At Home." *Education*, Vol. 78. No.4, December 1957, pp. 245-246.

Fiske, Edward B. *Smart Schools, Smart Kids*, New York: Simon & Schuster, 1991.

Fowler, William. "Cognitive Learning in Infancy

and Early Childhood," *Psychological Bulletin*, Vol LIX, 1962, pp. 181-283.

——. "A Study of Process and Method in Three-Year-Old Twins and Triplets Learning to Read," *Genetic Psychology Monographs*, Vol. 72, 1965, pp 3-89.

——. "Teaching a Two-Year-Old To Read: An Experiment in Early Childhood Learning," *Genetic Psychology Monographs*, No. 66., Chicago: University of Chicago Press, 1962. pp. 181-283.

Froebel, Friedrich. *The Education of Man*, trans. William Hailmann, New York: D. Appleton and Co., 1897.

Fromm, Erika, and Lenore Dumas Hartman, *Intelligence: A Dynamic Approach*, Garden City: Doubleday, 1955.

Gardner, Howard. *Frames of Mind*, New York: Basic Books, Inc., 1983.

Gerber, Richard. *Utopian Fantasy*, New York (McGraw Hill), 1973 (Orig. 1955).

Gesell, Arnold. *The First Five Years of Life*, New York: Harper and Row Publishers, 1940.

——, F. Ilg, G. Bullis. *Vision: Its Development In Infant and Child*, New York: Paul B. Hoebner, Inc., 1959.

Goins, Jean Turner. *Visual Perceptual Abilities and Early Reading Progress*, Chicago: University of Chicago Press, Supplementary Educational Monograph, No. 87, 1958.

Gould, Steven Jay. *The Mismeasure of Man*, New York: W. W. Norton & Company, 1981.

Gray, S.W., and Klaus, R.A., "The Early Training Project and its General Rationale," *Early Education*. R.D. Hess and R.M. Bear, eds. Chicago: Aldine, 1968, pp 63-70.

Greenough, William. Article in *Proceedings of the National Academy of Sciences*, Fall, 1990.

Gruber, Frederick C. *Foundations For a Philosophy of Education*, New York: Thomas Y. Crowell Co., 1961.

Harlow, Harry F. "Learning Set and Error Factor Theory," in Koch, editor, *Psychology: A Study of a Science*, New York: McGraw-Hill, 1959, pp. 492-537.

——, and Harlow, M.K. "Learning to Love," *American Scientist* 54:244-72, 1966.

——, and Harlow, M.K. "Learning to Think," Selection 22 in *Contributions To Modern Psychology*: Selected Readings in General. Dulany, Don et al., New York: Oxford U. Press, 1958.

Harvey, Neil (A.K.A. Harvey Neil Perlish, Ph.D.) "An Investigation of the Effectiveness of a Television Reading Program, along with Parental Home Assistance, In Helping Three-Year-Old Children Learn To Read, A Doctoral Dissertation," Frederick B. Davis, Ed.D., (Dissertation Supervisor), Philadelphia: University of Pennsylvania, (Microfiche-Ann Arbor, Michigan), 1968.

————. "Needed for the Eighties: A Mandate for Higher Order Literacy," *The In-Report*, vol. ix, No.3, May-June, 1981.

Havighurst, Robert J. *Human Development and Education*, Longmans, Green & Co., 1953.

Hebb, Donald O. *The Organization of Behavior*, New York: Harcourt, Brace and World, Inc., 1964.

Hechinger, Fred M. "1978 Freshmen Score Poorly on 1928 Exam," New York: *The New York Times*, March 18, 1980.

————. Education Column concerning Changed Lives, by David Weikart, New York: *The New York Times*, September 17, 1984.

Henshaw, Paul S. *This Side Of Yesterday: Extinction Or Utopia*. New York: John Wiley & Sons, Inc., 1971.

————. "Information Per Se," *Nature*, Vol. 199, No. 4898, pp. 1050-1052, September 14, 1963.

Herrick, C.J. *The Evolution of Human Nature*, Austin: University of Texas Press, 1956.

Hersey, John R. *Intelligence: Choice and Consent*, New York: Woodrow Wilson Foundation, No. 7, 1959.

Hess, R. D. "Early Education as Socialization," *Early Education*. R.D. Hess and R.M. Bear, eds. Chicago: Aldine, 1968, pp. 1-8.

Highet, Gilbert. *Man's Unconquerable Mind*, New York: Columbia University Press, 1954.

———. *The Migration of Ideas*, New York: Oxford University Press, 1954.

Hilgard, Ernest R. *Theories of Learning*, New York: Appleton-Century-Crofts, Inc., 1956.

Hirsch, E. D., Jr. *Cultural Literacy, What Every American Needs To Know*, New York: Vintage Books, 1988.

Holloway, Mark. *Heavens On Earth: Utopian Communities in America, 1680-1880*, London: Turnstile Press, 1951.

Holmes, Jack A. "When Should and Could Johnny Learn To Read?" Challenge and Experiment in Reading, *International Reading Association Proceedings*, Vol. 7., 1962, Fig. 1, J.A., Ed. New York: Scholastic Magazines, 1962, pp. 237-241.

Hunt, J. McVicker. *Intelligence and Experience*, New York: Ronald Press Co., 1961.

Huxley, Aldous. *Island*, New York: Harper & Brothers Publishers, 1962.

———. *Brave New World*, New York: Harper & Brothers Publishers, 1946.

Ibuka, Masaru. *Kindergarten Is Too Late*, New York: Simon & Schuster, 1977.

———. *Zero Years Old - Where Education Really Begins*, Tokyo: Goma-Shobou, 1986.

Kagan, Jerome. *The Nature Of The Child*. New York: Basic Books, Inc., 1984.

Kalil, Ronald E. "Synapse Formation in the Developing Brain," *Scientific American*, December, 1989.

Kasdon, Lawrence M. "Early Reading Background Of Some Superior Readers Among College Freshmen," *Journal of Educational Research*, vol. LII, No. 4, December 1958, pp. 151-153.

Krippner, Stanley. "The Boy Who Read At 18 Months," *Exceptional Children*, vol. 30, #3, November 1963.

Krogman, Wilton M. "Physical Growth As A Factor In The Behavioral Development Of The Child," in Walter Weejan, editor, *New Dimensions in Learning: A Multi-Disciplinary Approach*, Washington D.C., pp. 8-23, 1962.

LaBarre, Weston. *The Human Animal*, Chicago: University of Chicago Press, 1954.

Larkin, T. "Evidence vs. Nonsense: A Guide to the Scientific Method," *FDA Consumer*, June, 1985.

Laslett, Peter (Ed.). The Physical Basis of Mind, Basil Blackwell, Oxford Press, 1950.

Lazar, I, et al. "Lasting Effects Of Early Stimulation, A Report From The Consortium For Longitudinal Studies," *Social Research Child Development Monograph* 47, Nos. 23:1-141. (This report contains a very extensive bibliography.)

LeWinn, Edward B., M.D. *Human Neurological Organization*, Springfield: Charles C. Thomas, 1969.

———. "The Measurement Of Neurological Development," *International Journal of Neuropsychiatry*, vol. 3, no. 2, 1967.

———. "Effect of Environmental Influence on Human Behavioral Development," *New York State Journal of Medicine*, December 15, 1966.

Lerner, R. *The Nature of Human Plasticity*, New York, N.Y.: Cambridge University Press, 1984.

Lionni, Paul, Lance J. Klass. *The Leipzig Connection*, Portland: Heron Books, 1980.

Lorenz, Konrad. *On Agression*, New York: Harcourt, Brace & World, Inc., 1966.

McCracken, Glenn. "Have We Over-emphasized the Readiness Factor?" *Elementary English*, vol. 29, May 1952, pp. 271-276.

Margenau, Henry, David Bergami and the Editors of *LIFE, The Scientist*. Time, Inc. 1964.

Marler, Peter. "Early Patterns of Perception," *Natural History*, Aug/Sept, 1979.

Martin, Paul. "Kids Who Start Ahead, Stay Ahead," (an interview with Dr. Neil Harvey) *Chestnut Hill Local*, December 18, 1986.

Mayr, E. *The Growth of Biological Thought*. Cambridge: Harvard University Press, 1982.

MD Medical Newsmagazine, World of Medicine, vol. 22, no. 12, Dec., 1978.

Merton, Robert K. "The Self-Fulfilling Prophecy," Robert K. Merton, ed. *Social Theory and Social Structure*, New York: Free Press, 1968.

Miller, D. R. and G. E. Swanson. *The Changing American Parent*, New York: John Wiley, 1958.

Mithaug, Dennis E. *Self Determined Kids, Raising Satisfied and Successful Children*, Lexington, Massachusetts: Lexington Books, 1991.

Montagu, Ashley, Ed. *Sociobiology Examined*, New York: Oxford University Press, 1980.

Montessori, Maria. *The Absorbent Mind*, New York: Holt, Rinehart & Winston, Inc., 1967.

———. *The Montessori Method*, New York: Schocken, 1964.

Moore, Omar K. "Autotelic Responsive Environments and Exceptional Children," Special Report, Hamden: Responsive Environments Foundation, Inc., September, 1963.

———, and Anderson, A.R. "The Responsive Environment Project" *Early Education*. R.D. Hess and R.M. Bear, eds.. Chicago: Aldine, 1968, pp. 171-190.

More, St. Thomas. *Utopia*, Edward Surtz, S.J. Ed., New Haven: Yale University Press, 1964.

Morris, Desmond. *The Naked Ape*, New York: McGraw Hill, 1967.

———. *The Human Zoo*, New York, McGraw Hill, 1969.

Morris, William. *News From Nowhere*, London: Longmans Green and Company, 1912.

Mumford, Lewis. *The Story of Utopias*, New York: Boni and Liveright, 1922.

Murphy, Gardner. *Human Potentialities*, New York: Basic Books, 1958.

Myers, Garry. "Reading to Babies and Young Children," *Education*, vol. 77, May 1957, no. 9, pp. 516-579.

Nicholson, Alice. *Background Abilities to Reading Success in First Grade*, Ed.D. Thesis, Boston University, 1957.

Norton, Richard, Glenn Doman. "The Gifted Child Fallacy," *The Elementary School Journal*, vol.82, no. 2, January, 1982.

Orwell, George. *1984*, New York: Harcourt, Brace, Jovanovich, 1949

Osborn, Michelle. "More Choose to Stay Home With Children," Cover story, *USA Today*, May 10-12, 1991.

Parade, "Smarter & Wetter," September 23, 1979.

Peddiwell, Abner (Harold Benjamin). *The Saber-Tooth Curriculum*, New York: McGraw-Hill Book Co., Inc., 1939.

Penfield, Wilder, M.D. "The Uncommitted Cortex: The Child's Changing Brain," *The Atlantic*, vol. 214, no. 1, pp. 77-81.

—— and Roberts, Lamar. *Speech and Brain Mechanisms*, Princeton, N.J., Princeton University Press, 1959.

Piaget, Jean. *The Origin Of Intelligence In Children*, New York: W. W. Norton, & Co., Inc., 1967.

Pines, Maya. *Revolution in Learning*, New York: Harper and Row, 1967.

Plessas, Gus P. and Oakes, Clifton R. "Prereading Experiences of Selected Early Readers," *The Reading Teacher*, Vol. xvii, No. 4, January, 1964, pp. 241-245.

Rambusch, Nancy. *Learning How To Learn*, Baltimore: Helicon Press, 1962.

Ramón y Cajal, Santiago. *Recollections of My Life*, New York: American Philosophical Society, 1937.

Restak, Richard M., M.D. *The Brain: The Last Frontier*, Garden City: Doubleday & Co., Inc., 1979.

——. *The Infant Mind*, New York: Doubleday, 1986.

——. *The Mind*, New York: Bantam Books, 1988.

——. *Premeditated Man*, New York: The Viking Press, 1975.

Robinson, H.B. and Robinson, N.M. "The Problem of Timing in Pre-School Education," *Early Education*. R.D. Hess and R.M. Bear, eds. Chicago: Aldine, 1968, pp. 37-51.

Rousseau, Jean J. *Emile ou de l'Education*, Paris: Granier Frères, Libraires Editeurs, Also in Everyman's Library, Ernest Rhys, editor, Translated by Barbara Foxley, New York: E. P. Dutton, 1950.

Rowan, Helen. "Tis Time He Should Begin To

Read," *Carnegie Corporation of New York Quarterly*, ix, No. 2, 1961, pp. 1-3.

Sagan, Carl. *The Dragons Of Eden: Speculations On The Evolution Of Human Intelligence*, New York: Random House, 1977.

Scott, J. P. *Early Experience and the Organization of Behavior*, Belmont, California: Wadsworth, 1968.

Shaw, George Bernard. *Back To Methuselah, A Metabiological Pentateuch*, London: Constable and Company, 1921.

——. *Man and Superman*, New York: William H. Wise and Co., 1930.

Shister, Gail. "Norville now has baby and a radio show," *The Philadelphia Inquirer*, May 14, 1991.

Skinner, B. F. *Walden Two*, New York: The MacMillan Company, 1948.

Slevin, Jonathan D. "Geniuses Are Made, Not Born," *The World And I*, vol. 1, no. 10, October, 1986.

Sluckin, W. *Imprinting and Early Learning*, Chicago: Aldine, 1965.

Snow, C. S. *The Two Cultures and The Scientific Revolution*, New York: Cambridge University Press, 1959.

——. *The Two Cultures and a Second Look*, New York: Cambridge University Press, 1964.

Stapensea, Joanne. "Get Them Up And Running," *The London Free Press*, Canada, May 25, 1991.

Stapledon, W. Olaf. *Last And First Men*, New York: Jonathan Cape and Harrison Smith, Inc., 1931.

Stoner, Winifred d'Estecourte. *Natural Education*, Indianapolis: The Bobbs-Merrill Co. 1914.

Strang, Ruth. "Reading Development of Gifted Children," *Elementary English*, Vol xxxi, No. 1, January 1954, pp. 35-40.

Sutton, Marjorie Hunt. "Readiness for Reading at the Kindergarten Level." *The Reading Teacher*, January, 1964.

Suzuki, Shinichi. *The Suzuki Concept*, San Francisco: Diablo Press, Inc., 1973.

———. *Ability Development From Age Zero*, Athens: Ability Development Associates, Inc., 1981.

———. *Nurtured With Love*. Athens, Ohio: Senzay Publications, 2nd Ed., 1983.

Symposium on Brain and Mind. *Archives of Neurology and Psychiatry*, February, 1952.

Tabori, Paul. *The Natural Science Of Stupidity*, Philadelphia: The Chilton Company, 1959.

Tate, Merle. W. "Operationism, Research, and a Science of Education," *Harvard Educational Review*, vol. 20, no.1, Winter, 1950.

Terman, Lewis M. *Genetic Studies Of Genius*, vol. 1, Stanford: Stanford University Press, 1925.

Thomas, Lewis. "On The Uncertainty of Science," *The Key Reporter*, Vol. XLVI, Number One, Autumn, 1980. pp. 1-4.

Toffler, Alvin. *Learn For Tomorrow*, New York: Random House, 1974.

———. *Future Shock*, Random House, 1970.

Travers, Robert M.W. *Essentials Of Learning*, New York: The MacMillan Company, 1963.

Tyler, F.T. "Concepts of Organismic Growth," *Journal of Educational Psychology*, vol.44, pp. 321-342, 1953.

Van Dalen, Deobold B. *Understanding Educational Research*, York, PA: McGraw-Hill Book Co., Inc., 1962.

Walter, W. Grey. *The Living Brain*, New York: W. W. Norton, 1963.

Wann, Kenneth D., et al. *Fostering Intellectual Development Of Young Children*, New York: Teachers College Press, Columbia University, 1962.

Weikart, David. *Changed Lives*, Ypsilanti, Michigan: High Scope Press, 1984.

Wells, H. G. A *Modern Utopia*, London: W. Collins Sons & Co., Ltd., 1905.

———. *Men Like Gods*, New York: The MacMillan Company, 1923.

White, Burton L. *The First Three Years of Life*, Englewood Cliffs, N.J., Prentice Hall, 1975.

Whitehead, Alfred North. *The Aims Of Education And Other Essays*, New York: New American Library, Second Printing, July, 1951, Copyright 1929, MacMillan Company.

Wilson, Edward O. *Sociobiology: The New Synthesis*, Cambridge: Belknap Press of Harvard University Press, 1974.

Wolf, James. "Mother Goose Has Been Cooked," *The Minnesota Journal of Education*, January, 1968, pp. 12-15.

About the Author

Photographer, Joel Perlish

Neil Harvey is Dean of The Institutes for the Achievement of Human Potential. Dr. Harvey has a Ph.D. in early education, and is a Phi Beta Kappa graduate of the University of Pennsylvania.

In 1966, inspired by Glenn Doman's *How To Teach Your Baby To Read,* Dr. Harvey wrote, produced and appeared in 195 half-hour television programs, titled *Wordland Workshop,* on Channel Six, Philadelphia. This pioneer series, which preceded *Sesame Street* by three years, provided the vehicle for an historic study in which mothers, along with the TV show, helped their three-year-old children learn to read.

In 1979, the International Academy for Child-Brain Development awarded Dr. Harvey its coveted Statuette With Pedestal.

Index